Matt Hern, Am Johal
O My Friends, There is No Friend

New Ecology | Volume 9

Matt Hern is a founder and co-director of Solid State Community Industries.
Am Johal is the Director of SFU's Vancity Office of Community Engagement.

Matt Hern, Am Johal

O My Friends, There is No Friend

The Politics of Friendship at the End of Ecology

[transcript]

Bibliographic information published by the Deutsche Nationalbibliothek
The Deutsche Nationalbibliothek lists this publication in the Deutsche
Nationalbib-liografie; detailed bibliographic data are available in the Internet

First published in 2024 by transcript Verlag, Bielefeld
© Matt Hern, Am Johal

transcript Verlag | Hermannstraße 26 | D-33602 Bielefeld | live@transcript-verlag.de

Cover layout: Kordula Röckenhaus, Bielefeld

Print-ISBN: 978-3-8376-7026-4
PDF-ISBN: 978-3-8394-7026-8
ISSN of series: 2569-7900
eISSN of series: 2703-1039

Reading Matt Hern and Am Johal's 'O, My Friends, There is no Friend: Community at the End of the Ecology' is coming up for intellectual air and being able to breath in a radical and charged thinking space at a time when we feel suffocated by the enclosures of blatant simplifications in face of global catastrophes, the ecological devastations of global warming and of colonial and racial violence – both near and far. Matt Hern and Am Johal's sharp theoretical intervention reminds us of the lethality that is inherent to the kind of proximity given by the institutional holdings, such as the modern polity, the family, or the (ethnic or biologic or historic) community. And they do so while offering a map of the contemporary contributions to political philosophy from which we can draw a mode of being together – amity!! – without these fixed institutional holdings which cannot but rehearse separability and, with that, enmity.
– Denise Ferreira da Silva, Professor, New York University, author of Toward a Global Idea of Race *and* Unpayable Debt

In O My Friends, *Matt Hern and Am Johal search for a principle of solidarity unsubordinated to the nation-state and unbeholden to its policing of borders, respectful of identities but not of their enclosure. They find it in friendship – not as we think we already know it, but as an "elusive, allusive and aspirational relational form" still to be invented as a political practice. The book launches a passionate, thought-provoking call for the collective invention of a new sociality of concern and mutual exposure.*
– Brian Massumi, retired Professor in the Communications Department of the Universite de Montreal, author of What Animals Teach Us about Politics

Johal and Hern bring us a timely and inventive intervention when the political stakes couldn't be higher. We have not yet, or ever, solved the dilemma of friendship and community in times of crisis, but must return to critically examine their unique role and consequences to open up the potency of new radical political sequences and possibilities.
– Glen Coulthard, Associate Professor in First Nations and Indigenous Studies and Department of Political Science UBC, author of Red Skin, White Masks: Rejecting the Colonial Politics of Recognition

Contents

Acknowledgements

Some years ago, we started talking about the ideas that animate this book, and by mid-2019 they began to coalesce. We met weekly, or pretty close to that, at the Lido Bar or Portuguese Club, in Vancouver or Richmond: drinking, reading, writing and catching up without any timeline to stick to.

The following spring arrived and disheveled all our thinking. Our first chapter, "Staying Inside," was written pre-pandemic when we were blissfully ignorant of the absurd new set of meanings it would take on. We avoided writing about the virus, side-eying it from a safe distance, but it kept intruding, sneaking past our defenses, infiltrating our conversations.

As we wrote, we were also talking with anyone who had time for us as we tried to sort out our ideas. We were extremely fortunate that three people whose work we particularly admire: Jean-Luc Nancy, Leela Gandhi, and Leanne Betosamosake Simpson agreed to be interviewed – the book would have been very different without them.

One of the core questions we grappled with as we tried to pull our argument together was: How come so many people who write about friendship and community are such assholes? We got that question asked of us often.

This book is for all our friends and foes – but mostly our foes.

Special thanks is owed to these folks who directly contributed to our thinking and held our hands as we wrote: Joe 'The Crusher' Sacco, Julietta 'Jailhouse Rock' Singh, Willow 'Ecce Homo' Verkerk, Glen 'Motormouth' Coulthard, Amy 'The Queen' Kazymerchyk, Sanem 'Stylin' Guvanc, Hilda

'Take a Holiday' Fernandez, 'Jawbreaker' Jeff Derksen, Sabine 'Bad Ass' Bitter, Nermin 'Never Say Die' Gogalic, Daisy 'Educated' Couture, Sadie 'Orderly' Couture, Ashley 'Duchess' Dornan, Shane 'Torpedo' Trudell, Selena 'Mook' Couture, Althea 'The Whelper' Thauberger, Jerry 'Jay-Z' Zaslove, Ian 'Beef' Angus, Samir 'Boom Boom' Gandesha, Lesley 'White Lightning' Wood, Bruno 'The Blade' Marinoni, Erin 'The Spider' Silver, Christine 'Arugula' Atkinson, Jamie 'Four-Minute Mile' Hilder, Miyo 'Ribs' Takeda, Andrea 'Double Double' Creamer. This book is dedicated to our friend David Dennis who represented friendship, community and family to many people.

Much appreciation to Noema Magazine – where most of chapters 10 and 11 were originally published in article form, and to Pierre-Louis Mayaux and Max Rousseau for their translation help with Jean-Luc Nancy.

1. Staying Inside

It has been a particularly ugly start to the millennium. A bewildering groundswell of ethno-nationalisms, muscular forms of xenophobia and violent claims to territory have consigned planetary existence to a grid of highly regulated movement, enforcement of borders, expulsions, incarcerations and camps. The putative global order full of mobile freedoms is ordered by thickened borders, omnipresent surveillance and corpulent state administration of movement.

In late September 2019, then-U.S. President Donald Trump articulated this mood most starkly when he addressed the UN General Assembly, flexing the core themes of his presidency:

> The future does not belong to globalists, the future belongs to patriots [...] If you want freedom, take pride in your country. If you want democracy, hold on to your sovereignty. And if you want peace, hold on to your nation.[1]

Trump's bullying nationalism is a deformed extension of messianic fundamentalism that has its roots in the very formation of the state. The 1648 Treaties of Westphalia established a European (and now-international) political order based on the peaceful co-existence of sovereign nation states. While that juridical hegemon has been metronomically

---

1   'Trump at UN: 'The future does not belong to globalists. The future belongs to patriots.' American Military News, Sept. 24th, 2019.

punctured, it has held for almost four hundred years as a planetary order. Statism gives shape and substance to Us and Them and is the most potent available vehicle for belonging and expulsions.

This ordering labours to describe a managerial fabric of state sovereignties stitched together by international institutions, trading alliances, and globalization: a citizenry that knows its place, understands who is welcomed and who must be contained outside. Liberalism invokes a 'good nationalism' of beer ads, 'common-sense' immigration policy, the Olympics, World Cups and flag-waving nostalgia: a nationalism that doubles-down and reaffirms borders, defines 'the best of who we really are', and confirms our citizenship.

This citizenship is bound up with liberal cosmopolitan ideals of hospitality that assume an asymmetrical power relation where any migrant, anyone not 'from here' has to prove their worthiness for entry. It is a charitable idea, rather than one of justice. Hospitality, by its premise, has the capacity to be condescending, leaving the rights of others in the realm of arbitrary kindness – always contingent.

As twenty-first century borders are gored open by gushing flows of goods, capital, viruses and populations, this argument groans under intense internal and external pressures, desperate to bend, not break. Aggressive racial and religious-inflected nationalisms, opportunistic leaders and populist movements repeat old arguments: without strong borders there can be no nations. Incited by the viciousness of these new formations, liberalism can only yearn for borders that are a little less racist, cities that are a little more welcoming, governments that are a little more charitable.

This current crop of authoritarian xenophobes and military coups might well pass, but their point remains. Nation-states *have* to be built on identitarian exclusivity, an 'Us' keeping a 'Them' out. Without strong borders, nations dissolve. Contemporary forms of aggressive nationalism are not aberrations: they are new articulations of an extant form. Fascism is just nationalism taken seriously.

Borders never end. They are specific exercises of power that follow us everywhere. We might imagine that as we cross those cartographic lines, as we pass through, then the border is over. We breathe sighs of relief when the border guard finally lowers their gaze and waves us through, when our papers get stamped, when our applications are approved. But none of us are ever over or past the border – the inside is always subject to doubt and scrutiny. No one's legitimacy is ever safe, certainly never for migrants. We are all subject to constant management and zones of permanent administration that are now planetary in scale and reach.

These zones are functions and apparatuses of power that have a relationship to biopolitics and the management of populations, but are something new in their pervasive reach, suited for an era of ethno-nationalisms and ecological crises. They are accelerated by surveillance technologies and their ultimate resolution is carcerality, imprisonment, the camp – but these zones of permanent administration reach far beyond the human and are specifically deployed to adjudicate planetary movement.

These administrative zones are sometimes highly bureaucratic in the form of customs lines, visa forms, applications, and are sometimes violent and immediate like immigration raids, detention centers, Coast Guard patrols and camps. Often these zones are administered by dense webs of formal, official and state-sanctioned agencies, sometimes by quasi-official, semi-sanctioned and/or semi-legal government bodies. Far more pervasively, these organized efforts rest on the enforcement work of everyday people who administer belonging, citizenship and nationalisms.

The daily administration of movement operates ostensibly in relationship to borders but in reality saturates the entire life of a nation. The regulation and enforcement of citizenship demands constant vigilance against foreigners, overriding and re-coding everyday human relationships. The moral panics around foreign investors or anchor babies or hijabs are matched by vigilante border guards and everyday acts of violence towards migrants.

The nation-state is an inadequate rendition of community. All nationalist claims – and scaled-down localist renditions – demand borders and passports for entry. As soon as any 'inside' is marked off, there has to be an outside. Those definitions have to be rigorously maintained and policed, or else the distinctions between 'Us' and 'Them' dissolves.

But what are the alternatives? What other ways are there to be together? How can individuals and communities resist nationalisms with something other than entreaties for nations to be a little more just and inclusive? Can being-together exist without demanding constant rounds of expulsions? Can sociality be borderless?

The current globalized ubiquity of revitalized ethno-nationalism is a confluence of an imagined halcyon past of togetherness and the assertion of Westphalian national identity: blood, belonging and soil. To varying degrees, nationalisms are always cover for arguments about race and ethnicity – sometimes coded, sometimes overt, but easily surfaced. As the Wilsonian doctrine argued citizenship is always contingent on deeper fidelities, and every nation should be a state.

Consider this one example from our part of the world, a place steeped in its own mythologies of peaceful state multiculturalism. In February 1942, Canadian Prime Minister William Lyon Mackenzie King's cabinet, reeling from the Pearl Harbor attacks, issued an order targeting Japanese-Canadians. It was in the midst of WWII, and Canada saw an enemy lurking within. All through the country, and especially along the Pacific Coast, hidden in plain sight, in cities and lumber mills and fishing communities – were Japanese. Many of these people had been born in Canada and were citizens, some had been in the country for generations, many were children. Any person of Japanese ancestry was understood as a threat: they were captured, held in detainment, then sent to internment camps and work farms, their property and possessions confiscated and sold. Resistance meant confinement in camps hundreds of miles away. Every nation-state has stories of communities that have been persecuted in a form of collective punishment on the basis of religion or ethnicity.

Nationalist identity and belonging can be revoked under the most vague of threats to ethnic and/or religious paranoia and is repeated constantly on micro and macro scales. Repetitive events like Japanese internment camps, residential schools, Black land theft, Guantanamo Bay, Muslim homes burned, Rohingyans driven out of their villages, African students taken off the train leaving the Ukraine, migrant boats pushed back into the Mediterranean and a thousand other examples repeat what we all know in our bodies.

Take the example of our friend Nero, originally from the former Yugoslavia in the Balkans. He started in primary school, before the war, saying, 'Good morning, comrade' to his instructor until one day she came in and told them that they would no longer be doing that – instead, they would use the term *teacher*, one more suitable for their new political reality. When the civil war broke out in the early 90's and Yugoslavia broke apart, ethnic affiliation became paramount. As the conflict evolved, and new states formed in the region, Nero and his family became identified as Muslim in Croatia due to their last name and heritage, regardless of the fact the family didn't practice the religion. At every step, their identity was shaped by others without their consent. This made it impossible for them to claim an identity outside the one designated for them in the new geopolitical reality.

Every nation is founded on racial and/or religious identities, and here in the Anglospheric north, citizenship is always contingent on a proximity to whiteness. The 'We' that so many citizens fulsomely celebrate is inextricably bound to that identity. These are not malfunctions of identity. This is nationalism functioning on its very foundation. Every state on earth was borne out of some form of originary violence.

As nationalism continues to expose itself as profoundly inept at the task of being-together – of forging community – how else might we conceive of a 'we' and who is 'the people'? These are not questions of scale, or jurisdiction, or sovereignty, although those ideas thread through it.

We are after something far more pedestrian here. We want to know how to resist the claim that if you want freedom you have to have strong borders, and what that might mean in an era of ecological collapse. The logics of nationalism and accelerating ecological crises have the same root foundation: an inability to be together with others, human as much as the more-than-human. Thinking about ecology binds us to thinking about nationalisms and community. And how to think of the right to move and a right to breathe at a planetary scale that can think beyond the border?

This question of being-together haunts environmental as much as political thinking. The inability to imagine new renditions of being-together is how revived far-right movements, white nationalists and ecologists very often find common cause. Belonging is all good until you don't belong. Just because a community exists in common right now, does that mean that it needs to be so tomorrow? Community has never been immutable – it is constantly shifting, unstable and contingent.

It is impossible to escape the desire for being-together. What new ways can we be with humans and more-than-humans? How can we think past the state as the mediator of this question? We are asking here after a sociality that surpasses the limitations of the state, but it's more than that. How can we be-together where there are no entry fees, passports, borders or citizenship?

Our thinking on these questions keeps returning to friendship, an idea that has always appeared capable of surpassing nationalism, patriotism and the virulent claims of borders, always ready to permit passage. But friendship also tends to the trite and facile, a sickly call to individual cleansing and depoliticization. If thinking past borders demands a porosity and a freedom of movement that friendship gestures towards, is that enough to work with to imagine a non-statist sociality? Can friendship be the basis for being-together, for community?

2. Bound up

In the latter half of the twentieth century, arguments around 'community' re-erupted within continental philosophy's white patrician silverbacks, instigated in large part by Jean-Luc Nancy's book 'The Inoperative Community'. Others like Maurice Blanchot, Alphonso Lingis, Roberto Esposito, Georgio Agamben and Jacques Derrida piled on, and still others like George Bataille were revived and posthumously dragged back into the fray. These particular philosophical debates have largely returned to hibernation, but the urgency of the interrogation remains, carried forward in new languages by critical theorists, innovative philosophical movements, and more pressingly, by waves of migrants, activists, refugees, refusers and decolonial movements. The crises and failures of state-driven, authoritarian fascist and socialist experiments drove those discussions just as it had earlier in the twentieth century.

Speaking of 'community' is to ask after *sociality* – forms of being-together between humans and more-than-humans alike. The sociality we are after here is a fidelity that can escape both its familial and statist bonds, but we have almost no faith in contemporary commons literatures that whitewash over difference and history, a tendency perhaps most galling in environmental literature.

Facile claims that global warming somehow exceeds all difference and forges an 'anthropocene' where 'we' are all equally in peril and equally responsible to respond are precisely this: an aggressive depoliticization that obscures both the causes and responses and is as rude as any 'one world' or 'we are all in this together' rhetoric.

We can take heart from ecological crises. Not because we have hope that any catastrophe, emergency or quarantine is going to instigate widespread renunciations of extractive priorities, but these crises demand such jurisdictional reallocations and reorientations that a sweetness of life, of being-together, is imaginable, a new planetary world crawling out of the rubble of this one.

It's tempting to try and build an argument around the idea of *belonging*, to ask who belongs where? It is an easily-evoked environmental argument, that if we all felt that we really belonged somewhere we might take better care of the land we live on. Belonging has a close relationship to possession, to ownership. I belong here. This land belongs to us.

Belonging reveals a desire for permanence, for home, for fixity, for emplacement: a longing for, a be-longing, a renunciation of movement that calls for assimilation or expulsion. It betrays a desire for an extra-material transcendent connection to a place or a person. Belonging gives permission to the possession of territory and other bodies, gives us permission to push the boats back in the sea: those people do not belong here.

If we belong here – as so many localist politics claim is the benchmark for legitimacy – then it is *Us*, and only us, who can offer access to this place via permanent administration, assimilation, reconciliation and rights and eject those who do not adhere. It indexes, orders and reorients bodies, demanding and cataloging re-education camps and citizenship oaths. Belonging grants the power to contain, process, re-educate and/or admit. Building a politics around belonging doesn't sound like much of a world to live in, especially for anyone who doesn't belong, or is from somewhere else.

This idea of fidelity to the Fatherland, of exclusive claim to a place, threads through ethno-nationalist and religious fundamentalist arguments as easily as it does localist or ecological politics. This is precisely where revived far-right movements, nationalists and white environmentalism overlap and repeat one another[. The original Nazi party had a very comprehensive green platform. John Muir was an out-and-out racist who hated Indigenous people. John James Audubon was a brutal slaveholder and anti-abolitionist. Edward Abbey was an enthusiastic xenophobe and unapologetic racist, who called for hyper-militarized borders.

Certain strains of conservationists and environmentalists invoke similar hearth-and-home evocations of a nostalgic past to argue against immigration, for national control of borders as the only way to protect ecological integrity. This is not a malfunction of ideology; it is because their doxic narratives flow from the same fetishizations of togetherness. The evocation of conservative calls to family, homeland, and belonging are as useful to blood-and-soil politics as they are to localist environmentalism.

Listen, for example, to Marine Le Pen from France's National Front speaking about their ecological platform:

> Environmentalism [is] the natural child of patriotism, because it's the natural child of rootedness, if you're a nomad, you're not an environmentalist. Those who are nomadic [...] do not care about the environment; they have no homeland.[1]

This is startlingly similar to many localist arguments: a togetherness that accepts no punctures, no failing of identity, an essentialism that brooks no argument.

Much of continental philosophy attempts to chart a route beyond these movements by asking after an *inessential* community, a sociality that is not dependent on any essential quality. The best of these call for a 'community of people who have nothing in common' a being-together that is not yoked to nostalgic evocations of transcendence, nor the amelioration of personal anxiety or collective insecurity. This kind of in-essential being-together cannot be the product of a 'work' – it cannot be attempting to achieve, or un-achieve, anything, it can have no teleological essence – but can only bind people together through a desire for exposure, or vulnerability.

---

1   Oliver Milman, 'Right-Wing Climate Denial Is Being Replaced – by Nativism', *Mother Jones*, November 22, 2021.

Jean-Luc Nancy laboured to "invert the usual rational order in which community succeeds individuality" because any community that becomes "a single thing (body, mind, fatherland, Leader) necessarily loses the *in* of being-*in*-common. Or, it loses the *with* or the *together* that defines its essence. It yields its being-together to a being *of* togetherness." This loss is the foundation of all authoritarianisms and condemns "the political to management and power (power of management/management of power)".[2] This is the venom of all nationalisms, of all belonging. Being-together cannot accede to being fused into a single body or absorbed into a common entity.

As soon as anyone is sublated into a common, transcendent identity, they are no longer exposed, and thus lose the possibility of actually being-in-common: they exchange the porous exposure of being-together for the security of being-as-together, which is, of course, the move that all fascism, or nationalism, rests on. This is precisely where the political goes missing, lost in the fog of belonging – and 'politics' is rendered as disciplinary administration, management and border patrols.

The attraction of an inessential community is as palpable as it is pressing. The peril, of course, is that it hazards an embarrassingly romantic view of 'humanity'. In the context of innumerable years of pain, suffering and exploitive violence, any evocation of exposure, unworking, community without identity – or the more hipster 'horizontal affiliations' or 'human microphones' – runs the risk of aggressive depoliticization and a non-conflictual amnesia in the service of privilege.

When Nancy calls for a *community without unity*, or Agamben speaks of a *coming community*, those are unthinkable interventions, in the best and worst senses: it's so hard sometimes to imagine what that might entail. Desire for an inessential community, a commons or a communism without any entry fee is the proper refutation of nationalism as much as any yearnings for 'communities of shared understanding.' But an inessential community is also ready-made for erasure.

---

2   Jean-Luc Nancy, The Inoperative Community. University of Minnesota Press. 1991. 39.

After centuries of colonialism, unbridled racism and violent misogyny, the call to throw off identity in the name of community can sound assimilationist at best. It sounds like people who say that the colour of someone's skin doesn't matter to them at all, or they don't see race. Excluded and colonized people have every reason to resist any continued exposure to violence, and to dismiss fever-dreams of harmony or inessentiality.

Any organizing around notions of inessentiality immediately runs into the violence of racialized and religious expulsions. A borderless world is intensely appealing philosophically, but in the context of ongoing colonizations and ethnic cleansing efforts across the globe, bourgeois musings about inessential community are intensely perilous. Of course so many philosophers in the Western tradition are fixated on inessentialism – their essential identities have never been challenged.

Imagining new renditions of community beyond any transcendent identity is exactly what is required to surpass the violent nationalisms that stain our times. But this cannot float above the fray of the here and now, the everyday realities of deportations, dispossessions, drownings and incarcerations.

But a non-statist sociality – a utopian borderlessness – is not unthinkable, as Achille Mbembe implores. Utopian thinking is needed more than ever now. We are all always more than just our identities – and borderlessness requires us surpassing identity in ways that both affective and assemblage politics reach for. But we are all subject to the pain and weight of history and, in our estimation, utopianism should happily embrace essentialist identities – an intersectional politics that is not a transit point, nor a necessary evil en route to inessentialism – but as complementary ways of being in the world that are always bound up with one another.

In *The Coming Community*, Agamben tries to mind the gap by speaking of a *whatever singularity* – and in this case 'whatever' does not mean ambivalence or something that does not really matter, but the exact opposite. He speaks of 'whatever' as that which *always* matters. He explains his *whatever* thinking:

> Love is never directed toward this or that property of the loved one (being blond, being small, being tender, being lame), but neither does it neglect the properties in favor of an insipid generality (universal love): The lover wants the loved one *with all of its predicates*, its being such as it is.[3]

This seems to get us some of the way past the binding of inessentialism to erasure. We are interested in a community in which there are no conditions, there is no entry fee, no rent demanded, no work to be done, no passport to be shown. Where the threshold is a convivence that does not interrogate an essence, cares nothing for any citizenship, never asks for any papers. This makes imaginable a solidarity in incommensurableness – an inessentialism that does not require a shedding of identity but wants *all of it*.

But living in an age of ecological collapse, that formulation needs more. We are always exposed to the more-than-human, and to imagine a renovated ecology we have to mean being exposed to all of it, far beyond the human. We are exposed to animals and plants and oceans, but also to viruses and floods and fires and death, all of it – all the violence and injustice and cruelties of the more-than-human world. It is precisely an insipid generality that we have to refuse in the face of crises: we are not all in *anything* together. But we submit that the urgencies of ecological peril bring into sharp relief the idea of a community with no conditions: a borderless freedom to move, a refusal of recognition, a renunciation of any conditions – a time when no one has to drown in the Mediterranean.

In Derrida's estimation, exposure is at the heart of friendship – which is always bound up with grief. Being with a friend is always to simultaneously enjoy their presence and mourn their death. The pleasure of friendship is inextricable from the grief and loss of that friend. The only way to be-in-common is through exposure – exposed to finitude, exposed to death, and exposed to grief, or what he called the politics of

---

3   Giorgio Agamben, The Coming Community, University of Minnesota Press. 1993. 2.

friendship. We are particularly interested in what this means as we stare at the grief of a world dying around us.

As Willow Verkerk writes,

> For Nietzsche, agonistic relationships are formative of identities since people come to define themselves through the acknowledgement of their differences in opposition. The other spurs one on to greater performance and gives one the opportunity to examine one's selves through respectful competition. [4]

We are searching for a 'we' that is stripped of all its colonial, statist and anthropocentric fixities, one that can refuse to renounce identity while reaching for an inessentialism. This being-together has to be constantly exposed to the more-than-human. Community needs to extend far past the human if it is to retain any force: it has to think past species just as easily as beyond flags.

But if the first people we turned to here were Nancy, Agamben, Nietzsche and Derrida – we had better move quickly to get outside that continental tradition as well. As Sarah Ahmed puts it, that kind of thinking is really a 'reproductive technology', a "way of reproducing the world around certain bodies".[5] Maybe another way to ask the same question is to ask *who* is so fixated on 'community', and why? What's with all the hand-wringing? Continental philosophy is unapologetically fixated on who is in Europe and who is out – where are its borders located and why? But in whose interest is it to keep returning to these centripetal narratives of 'we're all in it together'? How can we escape the gravitational pull of these renditions of community and still imagine the politics of a borderless world?

Towards this project, we have started working from an astringent idea of friendship. Something that moves beyond definitional certainties. In the wake of Carl Schmitt, it is customary to suggest that if pol-

---

4   Willow Verkerk, Nietzsche and Friendship. London: Bloomsbury: 2019, 49.
5   Sarah Ahmed, Feminist Killjoys: Making Feminist Points https://feministkilljoy s.com/2013/09/11/making-feminist-points/.

itics are to have shape and meaning, we require enemies and friends. We come from a very different direction – the exact opposite direction actually – looking for a very different politicization, one demanded by ecological urgency.

3. Amity Lines

The long, slow unfolding of ecological crises makes the undoing of life legible in the present moment and forces us to vigilantly watch and count and extrapolate. The duress of human existence on the more-than-human world is felt viscerally and immediately, but at the same time – absurdly – somewhere far beyond these lifetimes, incomprehensible to daily cadences. Repetitions and echoes of old ways of being in the world are cocooned within dizzying pirouettes of denial and refusals of collective action.

Amidst the backdrop of collapse, there is an appealing tendency to reach into the far recesses of nostalgia, yearning for an originary thrown-out-of-paradise being-togetherness, a flailing kind of denialism cloaked in unapologetic romanticisms. Denial of death, denial of the crises, denial of the stakes, denial of the pain and suffering to come. This existence presents as surplus life, unnecessary life, wasted life – a necropolitics extrapolated to more-than-human lives amid calls to index and footnote the catastrophe to come.

If friendship demands exposure – if friendship is always necessarily entwined with the grief of losing that friend – what kinds of loss might be encountered at the end of this world: when it dawns on us that not only will we have to leave it, but now this world, at least in substantive part, will leave us, and is in fact leaving us now in an early and unjustifiable death?

As species and ecosystems cascade into extinctions, what happens if we cast our relationship with more-than-humans not as enemies, nor as supplicants to an abstracted Mother Nature, nor as kin – but as exposed to one another? The face of finitude is, ultimately, to be captured by an inside, by a being-in-common grief. If any ecology demands that we find good relations with the more-than-human, then why not as friends?

We live in an era that demands the very idea of nature come under interrogation. It is easy to claim that 'we' humans are destroying 'nature' but that formulation is unhelpful at very best. The more-than-human world is not helpless – it assaults us as callously as we do it, virally ending any idyllic reveries, demanding aggressive adjustment and defense just for us to get by.

As the ancient glacial fields melt beyond recognition, the world spins slightly off-kilter, off-pace, in new arrhythmias. The world can indeed go on without humans – and it will probably be better off and more interesting. Death denial as an act of self-preservation manages anxieties and excesses in myriad, dysfunctional ways including overconsumption, the accumulation of debt and addictions and technologies to manage disorders. And still, the world does not mourn us.

In rethinking and remodeling the work of togetherness today, we want to think beyond and around these closures of thought. The finitude of collective death cannot fuse a collective-in-finitude. Viral grief exposes us all, and not in any *we're-all-in-it-together* hallucinations. None of us are ever in *anything* together, distantly or otherwise, we are left to our bodily and corporeal exposure, to each other and to the more-than-human, just trying to survive.

The colonial state is permanently on a war footing: its prime directive is always self-preservation as an organizational form, and thus it is stuck in a permanent state of insecurity and frantic administration – constantly on defense against human and other-than invaders. Sovereignty is determined by who has the right to kill and who can determine who is disposable: a necropolitics that subjugates life to the power of death. What else are these fire-charred nightmares of global warming and sickness but necropolitics in everyday action?

The camp, the plantation, the reserve, the colony are outside, or an exception to the law by their very premise and are thus subsumed as part of the cultural façade and inertia of democracy. Mbembe argues that,"in these conditions, it might well be that, at bottom, no one is the citizen of any state in particular[...]. Becoming-human-in-the-world is a question neither of birth nor of origin or race."[1]

The question of freedom arises in the very act of distancing oneself from our places of birth or acquired nationalities: why does the randomness of our birth in a particular location determine our freedoms, including movement and the extent of freedoms we inhabit? What is the binding logic of the passport, the status card, the customs line?

Without movement, there cannot be politics, or as Hannah Arendt put it, movement is "the substance and meaning of all things political." The Soviet Union used to refer to itself as the homeland of socialism, but for Karl Marx, 'workers have no homeland': it cannot be the capture of belonging, but movement that politicizes the political.

It may have been disorienting at first to see mass-scaled anti-vaccination rallies throughout the pandemic featuring open fascists and white nationalists arm-in-arm with back-to-the-landers and conservation ecologists. The commonalities soon became clear: both camps rely on nostalgic fixities, renditions of a world-made-right, yearning for a time when people knew their place, when it was clear where everyone belonged, and fidelities were simple.

The intense management of movement between and within nations is a relatively recent phenomena – the modern passport was introduced only after WWI – but has grown so thick that states themselves are now zones of permanently administering bodies. The idea of freedom is bound up with the ethics of movement, of non-fixity, and is hardly foreign to any of us. Take queer subcultures for example who are constantly remaking every standard of being-together, dismissing all the disciplinary narratives of temporal inevitability, the 'progress' of heteronormative commands to monogamous coupling, cohabitation, property purchase, equity building, procreation, passing down generational wealth.

The never-satisfied, always restless, always hungry demands of progress and development can never abide by unworking, by any ab-

---

1   Achille Mbembe, Necropolitics. Trans. Steve Corcoran. Duke University Press, 2019, 187.

sence of success. The managerial directive *We are all in this together* is a blunt tool, most obviously disciplining the *we* and the *together*, but at least as importantly, fetishizing the *this*, eagerly optimizing virally reproductive isolations to enforce progress as an operational command. Exposure is weakness and you can never show your enemy weakness, especially to the more-than-human.

The upending of fidelity that movement demands suggests a new set of relations, one that does not retreat into nostalgic conservation nor teleologies of progress. Maybe the ecological crisis is itself a horizon of possibility – a landscape where no one ever needs a passport, a place where politics and good relations are indistinguishable from one another. The movement that freedom requires asks for new, unfixed ways to be-together.

What might a borderless world even look or feel like? The idea invokes constant negotiation, compromise, fluidity and non-fixity. It sounds like a certain kind of freedom, but also sounds insecure and unsettling, uncomfortable, wildly dangerous. Neoliberalism promises market liberty and a borderless freedom of accumulation, but simultaneously enforces a dense fabric of biopolitical control, aggressively policing and containing certain bodies with extreme prejudice. The neoliberal landscape simulates a certain kind of borderless world, but only for a privileged few, and predicated on thick borders for most.

The idea of borderlessness can be mobilized for many other kinds of purposes. Continuing American claims of Manifest Destiny have always ignored borders as justification for interference in the internal affairs of other countries, an unapologetic rationale for imperialism. Conversely, the border, in the face of muscular forms of state power, is also the defense against aggressive forms of power. Borders are often about protection – they are boundaries that lay down the line where power cannot cross, where identity is preserved and differences are maintained. Borderlessness is no utopia in of itself: in the actually living world borders serve many masters, but to think past nationalist closures, we have to think past those borders. The violence and existential threats of our times demand we imagine different ways to be-together.

The more-than-human world is marked by different renditions of borderlessness. Human observers have long presumed that animal territoriality mimics human regimes of private property – that animals all have distinct areas that they attempt to monopolize and defend from their own and other species. Ethologically that's a highly dubious proposition. It's far truer to say that members of a species have 'home ranges' they inhabit, areas that overlap with many other species that simultaneously practise co-avoidance and cohabitation with one another. The same holds true for non-animal species: there is evidence of what might be seen as territorializing behaviours among some plants, but animated by logics a universe away from anything most humans can recognize as familiar. The more-than-human world is built of innumerable overlapping and dynamic sets of space-use arrangements, relationships that are constantly being produced, negotiated and re-negotiated.

Humans are always producing territory, long before any performative lines on a map. The more-than-human world is constantly moving in fluid and borderless space, remembered, forgotten and renovated. We are not interested here in some romantic rendition of the more-than-human world and are not suggesting the rest of the world as some model for humans to sycophantically replicate. So much of the more-than-human world is awful and violent and deplorable: from murder and infanticide and cannibalism, to rape and pillage and abandonment. But we do want to suggest that the idea of borderlessness is hardly foreign to the human nor the more-than-human world.

It is our contention that our lived experiences of friendship might be able to provide some raw materials for thinking borderlessness. Friendship does not have to always be congenial or even friendly – it can be astringent and agonistic and malleable – but friendship is always voluntary, and thus always an exercise in agreement. We submit that any friendship, no matter its depth or breadth, is definitionally marked by a substantive concern for the other, which is the basis for the good relations that an ecological world requires.

Interview with Jean-Luc Nancy

Jean-Luc Nancy was a continental philosopher who wrote widely about many topics, including friendship and community. He published *The Inoperative Community* in French in 1986 and the English translation followed in 1991 – this was a seminal work that influenced our thinking in many ways and certainly helped us develop the foundations of this book. He taught at the University of Strasbourg, the European Graduate School and numerous other universities. This interview was conducted in May 2021, a few months prior to his passing and is recounted here, shortened considerably but with only light editing to reflect the tone and tenor of our conversation, at times allusive and elusive, and filled with flashes of insight. If he were alive, we may well have tried to edit this with him for additional clarity but hope this retains his particular flow and style of thinking.

AJ/MH: How do you think about friendship, community, *being-with* today?

JLN: Today, communitarianism means closure on a supposed identity, but the idea of communism, the word *communism*, came before Marx. It was an idealistic idea of politics for people who were at the time thinking a new form of society. The word communism expressed a consciousness, that something had been lost of the *being-in-common*. Even the meaning of common was lost. This is the reason communism became a word.

The use of the word has already been made without any reflection on what comes next, who with, and the means by which it comes about. It is clear that for the first people using the term after Marx, the starting point of the question of being-together starts before communism.

The point that was never examined in communism was precisely the content of the being *with*. In the whole history of Western philosophy, the *with* was never a question, was not answered. [...]. Aristotle says that to be together is not that simple, he speaks of the necessity of filia – like friendship, if you want. We could say from the time of Aristotle it was clear from all the Western tradition that society needs something, a certain force or energy to manage the *being with*.

And, why? Because I think we could say the whole Western ideal comes from the end of any kind of given community. There is, in the beginning of the Western idea, precisely the end of the way to make being-together possible. Maybe it's better to say this another way: to ask a question about togetherness.

Then the question is, what does it mean, *being together*? A mark, a sign, of the coming of the question in philosophy is in Heidegger. He brings up the question of being together in an ontological way as an aspect of Dasein – of existence. With Heidegger, instead of opening the way to think of another communism, Heidegger thinks in the way of an already-given community, the German people, and being-together becomes the struggle for the community of the people, *Volksgemeinschaft* later for the Nazis. Here are the origins of Nazism, fascism. Fascism has, in its own way, been an attempt to answer the question of community.

But at the same time and not by chance, in a reaction against socialism and communism, was individualism. It is nothing new – individualism was an invention of the Greeks, maybe more clearly emerging with Roman law. It is a technology to organize togetherness of something which was no longer people, but more than that. Under Roman law, everybody (though of course excluding women, slaves, foreigners), every 'citizen' was equal with the others. Equality is at the same time the designation of the individual as being something consistent by itself. From this time, the individual is for us, we could say, what remains of the end of the community and shall remain with a consistent link with others and the co-existence of the other.

But with Roman times, maybe at the same time with Christianity, the new link is a formal one of law. When it is not formal, when it is substantial, when it has content more than the formality of law, then it is in Christianity, where the individual is the son of God. We are all sons of God. Then it is something beyond the formal link of the law. But at the same time, it is not a visible link, and Christianity has answered this invisibility and sensibility, and the answer is Love. Love everybody and we are still without.

AJ/MH: You've started talking about the idea of friendship, referencing *filia*. Schmitt and Derrida claim that we need enemies to have politics. We are contending the opposite, that to think around that formulation is to reimagine a new kind of politics. We have begun to pull that thread a little bit, but friendship often has an insipid quality to it: we are looking for something more substantive. To what extent have you thought the political through friendship?

JLN: I don't know if I have a political conception of friendship. I understand what Derrida wanted to say and to think. I understand what it means precisely on the political level: there is no politics without friendship, but inside what? Inside a nation, state, people – all those walls are today in question inside, and outside there is a possibility of enmity.

But there are, for me, two questions: what is the unity of a people? A nation? It is not by chance today that we are so much in question, in trouble, in disorder about the identity of people. There is a necessity of having a new relationship of the people and how unified is the identity of a people. In Spain, you have Catalonia. Catalonia wants to be an independent country, because it has a language, a history, a culture – but what does that mean to make a country? We are putting into question the already given nations, which is absolutely normal as those nations are not eternal or ontologically constituted. This is a nationalistic way to think. I would say the modern idea of a nation is a very recent one, a very fragile one, absolutely normal to open questions. Today, economic and technical links are so strong that in a way, the idea of a national identity makes no sense. The Schmittian way of friendship and enmity is maybe now in a very different configuration.

My second question is: what does friendship mean? What is friendship? For Aristotle, *filia* is a goodwill for the other, *filia* is a quality or a virtue to discover, to be taught to your children, and it has to be cultivated by the citizen. What is at the core of friendship? I would say now, maybe after Christianity, we are more in a state to understand what is friendship, because love is the only common idea to all kinds of love – romantic love or Christian love – when we say love, we talk about relationship to other as other, the other in its otherness, like Derrida says, absolute otherness. Friendship is, in a way, a relationship with the same. A friend is the same to me. This is precisely the principle of the possibility of enmity. The other is to me who is not the same. We have the word In Greek, for otherness: barbarian, is the other. Barbar is a Greek word to name people unable to speak Greek.

It is not today a question about the sameness because we are no longer in a world where it is possible. How to think of the sameness in a political, or in a communitarian way today, how to think of sameness? I am the same as each of you using the same computers to make the same electronic relationships. We are the same because we are confronting the virus. With the virus, it is much more difficult to understand what it means to be an individual and to be a community. But of course we are individuals and each of us have individual consciousness and unconsciousness.

AJ/MH: We have two questions related to your work on friendship and community: How do you approach the ecological question in this context, and second, how do you view relationships between humans and the more-than-human?

JLN: I think the ecological question has now become philosophical – it has become more than an ecological question. Today, the problem is that the word ecology is an excellent word – but this word at the same time names something which remains like a specialty. We have to change that.

I think that there is much more at stake with ecology, precisely the meaning of technology. Because technology now is clearly the way that human activity and human production becomes an automated system or machine that produces its own means and goals. And then, it is a question about what we are doing in this world if there are people who are inventing some device to organize all my life, my food, etc.

Ecology is not only the question of nature, which is very important: the destruction or the quasi-destruction that we made or are making. It is more than the destruction of what would be nature. The question of nature is one of self-destruction. For somebody like me, with my age and old Western tradition, I cannot understand whether it is going to self-destruct or lead to revolution. Revolution is maybe an empty word. Maybe it will happen, that it will transform everything. Between the Renaissance and 19th century, all modern science and technology was created. It created a unique event, becoming a self-producing system which in a way is able to produce a mankind being entirely taken in this self-producing system.

The future is unknown and not possible to know in a sense. Or it is no longer a future. In French, we make a distinction between *futur* and *avenir* – *the future* and *to come*. The future is not known. On the contrary – the future is much more of a techno-scientific term, the future is a present projection for the time to come. It is not to come, it is already there. If I say, in fifty years it will be possible to produce life in laboratories, then the possibility by itself means that there are already all the means to go to this goal. In a way, the goal is already there. Of course, we don't know exactly in what way, but the future of the future is not the type of *avenir*, that is nothing is to come – everything is there, we saw that the past was given. We could now say that the future, as well, is given.

We invent new ways to keep people alive, but we have absolutely no idea of what that means – a long life. Why is a long life better than a short life? Nobody can say that. A long life is considered as something good, okay, because life wants to live. But in all previous cultures, it was presented together, the idea that life was to die. Today, we don't want to acknowledge that there is death. We find it difficult to deal with death.

AJ/MH: We have a question around nostalgia. One of the questions we've been grappling with is a non-teleological view of history, and you've drawn this tension between teleological and non-teleological ways of thinking in the wake of Heidegger. Similarly, you've drawn a distinction between regimes of production and non-production. This idea of *to come* – in particular in relation to teleology – is particularly interesting to us. In the face of these waves of exclusions and displacements, there's always a nostalgic time, a time of before, when community was true and wholesome. Can we think of community in a time that does not presuppose that we have lost community?

JLN: You are right – all this thinking about community, of communism, was based on nostalgia of something. Maybe there is an allusion of Marx which is that capitalism is producing a new form of life which will transform itself through an impulse of revolution in the teleological final status of humanity. Archaeology and teleology are linked together. That means that we have again to think out of this *archae, teleologics*. Then it means we have to think in the present, not in the present of today, for everybody and every people, the present of a life which has a certain duration, but during this duration it is less a place for production than for reproduction.

Maybe reproduction could be a word for ecology. Reproduction is a way of life. The way of life is to reproduce itself. Reproduction implies death. If there would be no death, there would be no need of reproduction. We understand reproduction as sameness.

Everybody lives, dies, but is that all there is? Maybe we could say that it all makes sense by itself. Without a need to expect something better tomorrow – that is a teleology. But how to understand that as an absence of any need for a better tomorrow – maybe that is all the problem – because maybe the now is not so good.

We have to invent a new possibility of reproduction. Maybe most rich people and the masters of technology are just living towards the future. Each of us has a relationship to reproduction – to death. But maybe it is only a melancholic relationship. Impossible to go away – a society cannot be melancholic as a structure. Because it goes towards suicide. We should not project the future change as reality, but as a dream. We have to dream. But what does it mean, to dream? We cannot only say that we are dreaming of a better tomorrow. We are dreaming, we are saying it's inconsistent. If we say a dream, then we come back to utopia. I agree it has a role, I would say a pedagogical role, maybe something more than a dream, that means not to make the dream come true, which is precisely the American way. From reality, the dream as dream, from the dream to something else.

4. What Are Friends?

We keep talking about friendship, but have been dancing around the question, avoiding taking it head-on. What is a friend? One obvious answer is that friends are not enemies, but that doesn't give us much room to move and boxes us in theoretically. Maybe a better starting point is to ask after the differences between friends and family, and whether that distinction gives us any political daylight.

Family is the past we were handed. Friends are freely chosen. Family is inescapable, friends are fluid. Families yoke us to all their failings and forgettable traits – all the more embarrassing because they are so obviously ours too. You can't do anything about your family, they stain every part of your essence, and everyone can see it plastered all over the way you talk, what you eat and the shape of your nose. It is as common to be chagrined about our families as it is easy to brag about our friends.

So why do people say their best friends are like family? Or that they are our brothers and sisters? Brothers from another mother. Sisters in arms. We are always comparing friends to family with metaphor and allusion, hoping that our friends are as close to us as family, just shed of all its patriarchal and historical baggage.

Family is seemingly the constant aspirational unit. Someone you can always call on. Someone you have to answer to, and who has to answer to you. People who will be there for you through decades. They were there when you were born and will be by your side when you die. Friends come and go, family is forever. You never have to prove yourself to your family, you are part of one another whether you like it or not.

Family is the antidote to all the anxious contingency and leakiness of friendship. But friendship is also the salve for everything that family saddles us with. Friends are a drink of cool water after a suffocating family encounter, the people who can talk us down and talk to us when we are down, who can understand us in ways our families never can.

But all this indexing is only useful in the most limited sense, and, like every binary, falls apart with the most gentle prodding. The flimsy designatory qualifications of who is friend and who are family are not categories – they are unstable, deferred aspirations.

The idea of family has been one of the most volatile and politically weaponized fault lines of the modern era. The political and religious rights have aggressively attempted to constrain definitions of family along nuclear lines, gender norms and role-fixities. This work is often relegated to culture war narratives, but it contains a more powerful undertow. The enforcement of family as an unimpeachable originary organizational unit is critical not just for what it claims, but for what it denies.

If movement is the substance of all things political, conservative renditions of family are fixated on preserving borders, and leakiness is perilous. Attempts to broaden or muddy the family waters are viciously resisted as somehow emperilling the form. But frantically trying to concretize family is wildly ahistorical and runs aground of almost all our lived realities. Consider how so many of us use *Auntie* and *Uncle* to refer to almost any older person. Or how so many cultures use 'cousin' or 'cuz' for most anyone close to you – maybe or maybe not of any direct relation. Think how many people – and animals – who you share no direct blood with – have been unequivocally part of your families over the years.

There are endless other generous renditions of *family* everywhere, and any attempt to fix the form in place inherently reduces it. The more open the idea of family is, the more powerful it becomes. Porous and flexible renditions of family do not weaken it, they celebrate it. The desire to lock 'family' in place is a close ideological sister of moves to nationalism, racializations and gender binaries.

The opprobrium directed at trans people from seemingly otherwise reasonable commentators is as confounding as it is awful, and one possible explanation is a fearfulness of any fluid freedom of movement – a freedom that echoes evocations of borderlessness. Political and religious conservatives tend to fear and loathe migrants and trans people equally, and for related reasons: a surpassing of carceralities, the horizons of new possibilities and fracturing of certainties. Xenophobia and transphobia are not equivalents, but there are clear correlaries between the desire for certainties that animates them. This is the ocean that friendship swims in. Family and friends are not synonymous, but what is the point of trying to definitionally constrain either?

The work of indexing and cataloguing friendship has been as strenuous as the attempts to mark off the borders of family. Studies of friendship in the western philosophical tradition almost always start with Aristotle. Which is expected: *philos* is the Greek word for friend, both have etymological relationships with *freedom*, and in many ways all philosophy is grounded in thinking about friendship. As Agamben put it in 2017: "Friendship is so tightly linked to the definition of philosophy[...] that without it, philosophy would not really be possible".[1]

Aristotle called friends 'another self' and taxonomized friendship into three types – those of pleasure, of usefulness and true friendship, and concluded (in part) that "without friends no one would choose to live, though he had all other goods". Following his lead, thousands of years of philosophical exploration and near-endless attempts at ordering have worked and reworked these categories, organizing and reorganizing taxonomic species, genus, class and phyla of friendship, and gauging their various worths.

It is tempting to try to articulate the nature of 'deep' or 'true' or 'meaningful' friendships, if only to perhaps be able to better understand how they are formed and lost. But we are convinced of friendship's fundamental ineffability. Friendship *has to be* a slippery, porous and contingent concept: by definition it has no easy definition, no easy borders. Julietta Singh keeps reminding us not to try and capture the idea: "friendship

---

1   Giorgio Agamben, 'The Friend', in What is an Apparatus?, Stanford University Press, 2009. 25.

is the name we give to relationships for which we have no other stable name".[2]

There is no question that friendship is a surpassingly elusive, allusive and aspirational relational form – and that lack of definitional clarity is no lack. The capaciousness of the idea is the field where we can contemplate borderlessness, and still, we have to be able to carve out space for talking about the idea. It is not enough to claim it and refuse it in the same breath. It is wholly possible to talk about the shape and substance of friendship without reverting to building a definitional wall: the territory is in the making of it.

We are certain that friendship is always voluntary and consensual. Rationales for who is and is not a friend are never rational – our affections are so often capricious. Friends do not have to be sweet or kind or generous to one another, they don't even have to be friendly, but they do have to have substantive concern for the other's welfare, and they do have to consent to be friends. Friendship is always an exercise in agreement.

One of our main goals here is to extend the customary evocations of friendship as occurring between two people and ask after collective friendships – gesturing towards the notion of shared happiness. As much as we are curious about the political potentialities of interpersonal friendships, we are equally interested in recalibrating our political ontologies, or maybe to ask: can one group of people be friends with another group, even a more-than-human group? If states have proven themselves inept as apparatuses of community, how can friendship lend itself towards other ways of being-together, ones that might be tenable in a time of ecological collapse?

Towards that, there are three threads that we want to pull on. First, is the seemingly foundational and oft-evoked notion of friendship as requiring substantive concern for the other. Theorists of friendship often settle on this as a bland enough launch point, but it strikes us as a simple formulation at the heart of all aspirationally ecological thinking. A 'substantive concern for the other' is the antipode of the grooved orthodoxies of exploitation and extractivism.

---

2   Personal conversations, October 2021.

This 'substantive concern' is reversed in a fun way when we consider the extreme awkwardness of unrequited friendship. It may be that 'unrequited love' is an essentially stupid idea, but there is at least conceptual territory there, buttressed by endless evocations of love/lust/infatuation being unacknowledged/unreturned. Unrequited friendship is embarrassing in that substantive concern for the other is what makes friendship possible: it is not enough to claim someone as friend, they have to claim you back.

Second, we want to stay with the necessarily voluntary character of friendship, closely related to requitedness. Friends have to agree to be so. If friendships are always freely chosen, then they are also shifty and up for grabs. Friendships are constantly being ordered and reordered, lost, refused and revived: we always have to prove ourselves. The borders between acquaintance, friend, good friend, close friend, best friend, bff – and all the subtle distinctions within – are never fixed. Those commitments require us actively maintaining, making, remaking, and evaluating them, and while it may be nice to think that we can rely on certain friends forever, that doesn't work out all that often. That reality is somewhat unsettling, but the instability of friendship is not regrettable, it demands effort and political fidelity.

Third, friendship is a conspiracy. Even in its porosity, it is a private, restricted affair to which invitations are obtuse, and entry is a closely guarded secret, sometimes even to our friends. The trust that conspirators require can always be violated and/or withdrawn, sometimes for the flimsiest, most inscrutable of reasons. Final decisions about who is a friend and who is somewhere in-between are always deferred. But equally, those invitations open and welcome without warning – we can make friends sometimes almost instantly, sometimes we make great friends just for one evening, sometimes for reasons we cannot explain. The act of inviting someone to sit at the table to share a drink, or into the kitchen for a meal is to think past borders, closing distance and hazarding leakiness.

Friendship has nothing to do with morality, which has pretenses to the universal. We treat friends differently with no apologies, offer favours and gifts and time and tolerances that we would never dream of offering anyone else. This makes friendship aesthetic: it is valuable not because it is moral, but because it is beautiful, and thus always experimental. In this creativity, friendship is always making and unmaking worlds.

In its porous and shifting exclusivity, the political horizons of friendship can push democratic theorizing past its colonial fixities, but at the same time every assemblage of friends has to account for itself. Neither friends nor enemies are static. The enemy can be turned into a non-friend or a friend. Or real enmity can be turned into absolute enmity in the case of war and hand-to-hand combat to the death. Friends and foes are always fluid designations.

There is an easy leap for some to see friendship as redolent of accounts of brotherhood and fraternization, and as much as the vision of assemblages constantly moving and flowing, rhizomatically coming together and reassembling across smooth spaces is beautifully attractive – those assemblages hazard grooving the same patterns of exclusivities, re-enacting the world as it is over and over again.

If decolonization can be perceived as an event, or as Mbembe puts it, as "an active will to community", then how might an 'active will to friendship' offer routes to think politics differently, to imagine what kinds of new formations borderlessness might instigate? And how might friendship be untied from its anthropocentric moorings? Or: how can friendship help us put fire to the colonial fixities of 'we'?

In Nancy Sherman's estimation, friendships are relationships that structure the good life, a mode of good living that is necessarily bound to the happiness of others. That experience of substantive concern for the other, of recognizing the happiness of one is essential to the happiness of any and all, is solid footing to build a politics that apprehends a borderless community.

5. What Are Politics?

There's no question that the idea of a borderless world appeals to some quixotic impulses. A time without borders sounds like freedom, or something akin to it. No more passports, no more detention camps, no more expulsions and deportations, no more ICE or Brexit, no more putatively decent people pushing boats of starving refugees back into the sea.

But any instigation of borderlessness is perilous. The market fundamentalism of neoliberalism loves the elimination of trade barriers as its own form of borderlessness. Late capitalism cheers the freeing of corporate flows of capital through and across nation-states for transnational accumulation, but aggressively denies that same freedom of movement to people. That version of borderlessness leaves most of us trapped in confounding spiderwebs of capture.

Where there is a border, there is aways a political community in flux – never fully formed, never solidified and whose membership is liquid and prone to the possibility of suspension, dissipation, and possible exile – all in the name of fixity and solidity. The production of inferiority creates constant unabating anxiety about whether one deserves to be there or not, whether a knock on the door or a phone call will turn one's life upside down. It is a characteristic of the permanent state of order and disorder where one's status can always be taken away.

Crises of ecology and economy have inevitable inertias that lead to extreme localism as a possible intervention to global capital flows and domestic inequalities. Calls for direct democracy and organic forms of decision-making have populist appeal on the left and right. The calls for economic nationalism at a broader scale against global capital can tie disaffected populist voters with progressives, anarchists and socialists in a shared critique of the state.

The local place versus the rootless cosmopolitanism evoked by the *somewhere* versus *anywhere* articulations of political community mobilizes resentment of the individualizing brutality of hollowed-out neoliberal economies. Those who are exiled from somewhere to anywhere, cast out by economic flows, or the reverse, are hardly beneficiaries in this violent binary.

In this context, the politics of belonging that tie these disparate strands of environmentalism, planning and retreatist localism together in its complacently Western form is the most pernicious of identity politics that cuts across class boundaries – *whiteness*. But it is also mobilized in new nationalist and majoritarian forms from India to Turkey to China to Yemen to Brazil, constructions that reach beyond white nationalisms and into new forms of racial-religious belonging.

When we consider bare life and the social relations of inequality that shape these conditions of belonging and expulsion, we have to consider the broader question of human and more-than-human, moving beyond the anthropogenic threshold. Self-preservation is increasingly bound to the more-than-human at a planetary level. To move beyond the limited scope of the self, to see shared flourishing as a precondition of the political, and to then extend that to the more-than-human, raises the stakes of pre-emptive miscommunication. What is at stake is a present-day being-togetherness that has the capacity to be a form-of-life – one that has the capacity to resist the inequities of the world as it is, but refuses a unity at every step.

We are bound by the possibility of a community that has the capacity to both deny and overthrow power. This is not to name an enemy to stand against but must, by its very possibility to form and cohere, be an affirmative construction that can overcome the limits of its threshold. The line can never be clearly demarcated – it is intended to be amorphous, dangerous, contradictory, porous, leaving traces of an inside and an outside, borderless but stubborn, refusing to be enemies.

Through friendship, both inside and outside are forced into new relations. These are not fixed, frozen relations, but malleable, open to dis-
agreement, disarray, dissipation and with the possibility of concretizing affect in the realm of the public and the intimate. To be-together in
friendship is simultaneously an articulation of freedom and duress. It
is the place of gossip, teasing and tenderness of being close and being
closed – a relation without purpose, but moments away from the possibility of mobilization and/or dissolution, and a constructed purpose
from without. In our estimation, this is the best rendition of 'the political'.

Politics that are bound by the friend-enemy distinction are disastrously limited – at their most banal, they become management of borders and exercises of sovereignty and jurisdictions. Politicizing politics
needs to rest on a much more nuanced set of relationships – friendship
as one possible route and one we all have experience with in the everyday – politics as negotiation, compromise, consent, argument, and
agreement.

In 'The Murmuration of Birds: An Anishinaabe Ontology of Mnidoo-
Worlding' Dolleen Tisawii'ashii Manning asks what a bird sees when it is
flying in a flock, in a murmuration. How do starlings turn apparently
suddenly, but all together without colliding, how do they create these
beautiful, interweaving, cascading patterns without ever getting in each
other's way, running into one another, how do they know how to move?
She calls this an "all-encompassing and interpenetrating mnidoo co-re-
sponsiveness":

> The result is a resistance to cooption that concedes to the heterogene-
> ity of being. I define this murmuration, that is, this concurrent gather-
> ing of divergent and fluctuating actuation/signals as mnidoo-world-
> ing. Mnidoo-worlding entails a possession by one's surroundings that
> subsumes and conditions the possibility of agency as entwined and
> plural co-presence.[1]

---

1   Dolleen Tisawii'ashii Manning, "The Murmuration of Birds: An Anishinaabe
    Ontology of Mnidoo-Worlding." in Feminist Phenomenology Futures, Eds. He-

This 'plural co-presence', like every sophisticated rendition of het-
erogeneity/gathering is almost unthinkable in the context of colonial
fixities.

When community is contained with borders – nationalist or otherwise – any creative instabilities are occluded behind a veil of imagined
fixity and ethno/racial/religious ordering. If we are going to assert that
the political is necessarily non-processual and non-teleological, then
identity and affect require one another, stitching together intersectionality and assemblage as 'convivial modes of thought'. Intersectionality
ruptures dead-end forms of political closure and becomes porous and
inconsistent at the moment of exposure. We are curious about the origins of power that can break the bonds of community and undermine
the tenuous, sinewy capacity to resist. Proximity to others can mean
helping hands or choking one's breath away.

If one of the origin points of being-together is to preserve collective
life, can this be done without the border? The stranger is someone we
do not know but may be open to. The intruder/stranger is named and
can never be welcomed, forever banished, shunned and in exile within
and without. Pluriversalities and emancipatory political struggles are
attempts to redraw this link as the basis for a community organized
around the possibility of a political outside, which also has a solidaristic
motivation to the more-than-human. But power and authority still have
the capacity to authorize, designate, decide, index and overwrite the
political force of any given community.

Identity and politics intersect where the filtering, sorting and designation of people by passport becomes the most rudimentary inscription.
Moving towards dehumanist solidarities is to democratize relations with
the human and the more-than-human simultaneously outside of mas-
tery. Politics is engaging in a deliberate composition of the future beyond
colonial exhaustions.

The strain and tension of friendship gives texture and character to
the capacity for this futural orientation. Politics is a movement to stand

---

len Fielding and Dorothea Olkowski, Bloomington In: Indiana University Press,
2017.

up on one's own and build community in the realm of exposure with the other. Politics is where human implication with the more-than-human requires constant uncertainty, social volatility, contingencies and accidents. This is to build a dialectical relationship that brings the more-than-human to a site of exposure where radical democracy and justice can be contemplated. Politics is reimagining the contours of community beyond territorial bounds and technological apparatuses, and actively willing oneself into the uncertainties and instabilities and compromises of exposure.

Resisting any unified accounts of the universal human allows us the specificity that is imperative in understanding the relation to exposure and other forms of life. It is part of the stretching, elasticity and plasticity required to shape a future world collectively. If democracy means anything at all as a site of the political, it is always already a democracy-to-come, one that includes all of us, everyone outside the bounds of legibility, human and the more-than-human, bound up in our very capacity to think the future together.

The ongoing production of inferiority fuels the machine of colonialism. We need to reimagine the composition of politics beyond an anthropomorphic straitjacket. The inevitable movement of politics is to do away once and for all the false division of beings who act and those who are acted upon. The violence and authoritarianisms that attempt to establish order are a symptom of the reactionary void and wound.

If we reduce politics to the State form, to the defense of the sovereign, we can only reduce ourselves to nationalist jingoism that rudely undermines the possibilities of being-together. The most durable route to community has to be through a politics of exposure, to do away with domination as mode-of-life and imagine a present and future as new relations. The political is the will to life and the movement of choosing living over surviving.

6. Staking Claims

How can it be that anyone *belongs* anywhere, or to anyone? It fixes people in place, polices movement, tells us where to be, and permits expulsions. All nationalisms lean heavily on the idea that the world-made-right requires people to return/be returned to their rightful places, the places where they belong, for everyone to go home. Every border checkpoint, every passport, rests on the notion that certain people belong on certain lands, and maintenance requires the constant enforcement of that catalogue.

But if decolonization is to have material, non-metaphorical force, resistance to occupation starts with reclaiming land and asserting who can and cannot lay claim to it. Indigenous people across the globe demand the return of stolen lands, and the agency to determine who does and does not have access. Post-coloniality has always rested on the return of land to its previous inhabitants: without land, Indigenous peoples cease to exist, and any desire for inessentialism has to chart a route that simultaneously abhors and embraces borders. Invocations of community can never be disembedded from four hundred years of colonialism and abstracted notions of being-in-common are always subject to imperial hunger.

Colonial genocide, occupation and domination surround us all, and how we think of being-together always breathes that air. It might be that strategic, or corrective, essentialism is the only route to inessentialism, but that seems dismissive or patronizing to intersectional politics. Nationalism is always toxic, except when it is not. Belonging and membership is never an argument for being-together, except when it is.

The weight of colonial depravities requires constant resistance even (especially) from people who name themselves 'allies' or people who claim to belong. Take US Senator Elizabeth Warren, for example. For decades she has very effectively muddied the waters around her background: implying, stating, suggesting that she is Cherokee, has Cherokee heritage, is Indigenous, or something like that. For decades Warren was very careful publicly with her claims, and always left a few obfuscatory routes of escape open, but if it seemed worth it, she happily just lied. When she was faculty at Harvard, she listed herself as a 'minority law professor' and when she registered for the Texas State Bar, she identified her race as 'American Indian'.

When confronted about these claims, Warren always rope-a-doped, saying she knew she was Cherokee because her grandma always said they had a relative, or that it was a family story that she had no reason to question. As her run for the Democratic presidential nomination gathered steam through 2018 however, scrutiny and sneering accumulated from both sides of the aisle. Far more importantly, Cherokee scholars and leaders demanded she come clean. She kept retreating, fighting rearguard battles, avoiding real confrontation, until – disastrously – she took a DNA test, and then trumpeted the results that 'strongly supported' the existence of an Indigenous ancestor six-to-ten generations back.

She was quickly – and very publicly – informed of her mistake, and then privately reached out to the Cherokee Nation to express regret for 'causing confusion', but still did not seem to grasp just how wrongheaded her attempt to appropriate identity was. Warren continued to spin the situation, and in 2020 more than 200 Cherokee and Indigenous signees wrote an open letter demanding she 'fully retract' all her previous claims, work to dispel the myths she helped spread and ameliorate the damage done. They noted the massive theft of public funds by white people feigning Indigenous identities:

Claiming Native identity without citizenship, kinship ties, or recognition from Native communities undermines Indigenous self-determination. As the most public example of this behavior, you need to clearly state that Native people are the sole authority on who is – and who is not – Native.[1]

Warren responded promptly, returning a twelve-page letter that retreated a few more steps, acknowledging that she is white, and offering: "I was wrong to have identified as a Native American, and, without qualification or excuse, I apologize."

She then immediately qualified and excused herself, claiming she "never benefited financially or professionally" (which is another lie) and then didn't miss the opportunity to carefully detail her campaign's policy platform that she said would be good for Indian Country.

Ok, fine. So what if a politician is a little loosey-goosey with the truth, and indulges in little play-acting here and there, especially when she is apparently a good, progressive person? The problem of course, is that this line of analysis centres precisely the wrong things and people. As Cherokee artist and writer Rebecca Nagle says, the real issue is colonial occupation and Indigenous survival:

> The center of this controversy is not Warren's political career, it is Cherokee sovereignty and self-determination. The monster I am trying to wrestle to the ground is not one white woman who claimed to be Cherokee. It is the hundreds of thousands of white people claiming to be Cherokee and the broad social acceptance that emboldens them. It threatens the future of my tribe. Warren is just the most public example.[2]

It is important here that perhaps the key fulcrum in this story was Warren's reversion to a DNA test to 'prove' her claim of ancestry. It is a very common tactic, and one that seemingly should settle things: science and genetics to the rescue, bearing objective truth to answer questions of who *belongs* where and to whom, and permitting oneself passage.

---

1   'An Open Letter to Elizabeth Warren', Medium, February 26th, 2020.
2   Rebecca Nagle, 'Elizabeth Warren Has Spent Her Adult Life Repeating A Lie. I Want Her To Tell The Truth.', HuffPost, 2019.

Joseph Boyden tried this too. Boyden is a best-selling Canadian writer, who like Warren, is a powerful, highly accomplished public intellectual who has cut a prominent figure supporting progressive causes, particularly around Indigenous issues. In familiarly slippery ways, Boyden has claimed all kinds of ancestry, from Mi'kmaq to Nipmuc, Metis to Anishnabe, Ojibway to Huron-Wendat, strategically landing on the phrase (after many years of questions) that he is a white kid with native roots' and that "a small part of me is Indigenous, but it is a huge part of who I am."

Although there had long been whispers about his identity, Boyden's case drew increasing scrutiny as his profile grew, and by 2016 he was being forced to openly defend himself. Unlike Warren, who has a long and varied career, Boyden has staked all his writing and legitimacy on nonsensical and shifting claims to Indigeneity, and so has fought back hard, despite his record of dubious claims and outright lying. One of the key pillars of his argument was the DNA test he took showing some (unclear how much) Indigenous ancestry:

> If I am accepted by people in Indigenous communities, if I have been traditionally adopted by a number of people in Indigenous communities, if my DNA test shows I have Indigenous blood, if I have engaged my whole career in publicly defending Indigenous rights as well as using my public recognition as an author to shine light on Indigenous issues, am I not, in some way, Indigenous?[3]

It's now broadly accepted that Boyden is a charlatan who built a lucrative career playing Indian and got away with it for a long time, like so many Grey Owls before and since. But he remains strategically-adept and the title of his major in-defense-of-himself essay was 'Being Indigenous isn't all about DNA. It's about who you claim, and who claims you' – ironically-enough given that one of the central claims of that essay was his DNA test.

---

3   Joseph Boyden, 'My name is Joseph Boyden'. Macleans Magazine, August 2nd, 2017.

There are a surprising number of other high-profile examples of these deceptions and surely will be many more to come. It's a little hard to see how it's possible for people to pull these deceptions off given the extraordinary levels of public access to information, but people like Rachel Dolezal have taught us that identity falsifications are hardly limited to Indigenous facades. There are so many versions of the same basic move, from adopting a 'Black' accent, to inventing a gangster past, to writing best-selling autobiographies feigning being a Holocaust survivor. The motivations are sometimes obvious (receiving awards and grants) other times seem to be ineffable, flailing attempts at authenticity (or something?) – say some D-list celebrity faking a Spanish accent despite being raised in Boston.

No matter whether the implications are profound or inconsequential, there is always power in play. If the two of us writing this book decided to claim to be Irish all of a sudden, no one would really care all that much, frankly. It's just not true, and it would be kind of weird if either of us were to make that claim. One of us has something of a better argument to make, but honestly it would pass with little notice and it would barely move any needles for anyone. It is however really important to talk about who gets to claim Indigeneity with material consequences, such that some prominent Canadian Indigenous people are now calling for fines and/or jail sentences for Pretendian misrepresentation. There is precedent: the U.S. Indian Arts and Crafts Act of 1990 makes it illegal to falsely claim that any item was 'Indian-produced' and even a first-time violator is subject to a $250,000 fine and/or up to five years imprisonment.

In many communities and settings it is customary to introduce yourself by speaking of your parents and grandparents, aunts and uncles, acknowledging your ancestors and where you, and they, are from. It is a way to root yourself, for others to understand who you claim and who claims you, and who your families are. It is a practise that is echoed and emulated in many different ways and circumstances. It tends to have a subtly flustering effect on settlers when they are asked who their people are. White people never think they have to account for themselves, they think they are from everywhere, and deserve to be anywhere and everywhere.

Colonial apparatuses have tried to steal not just land and offspring, but the capacity to adjudicate who is and is not Indigenous, and decolonization demands that Indigenous people are able to define membership using whatever criteria they decide on. But even that gets fraught, because colonialism has stripped many Indigenous people of membership and connection to their families through deliberately genocidal policies. Undoing the rubble of colonial deprivations keeps revealing layers of devilish complexity, but it is certain that there is no route past nationalism without foundational assertions of Indigenous identity.

It is not enough to be able to claim Indigenous or other heritage, someone has to claim you too. People unilaterally claiming Indigeneity are always embarrassing disasters because no one has claimed them back – they are living in a solipsistic fantasy. Friendship echoes this kind of reciprocity: friends have to claim one another as such, each party has to consent, and each has to have a substantive concern for the other. That seems like the foundation for any good relationships.

Kim TallBear, maybe the most prominent researcher in North America of scientific attempts to establish Indigenous heritage and author of *Native American DNA: Tribal Belonging and the False Promise of Genetic Science*, often frames questions in terms of good relations. Speaking of Elizabeth Warren, she said:

> To be a relative, you have to actually spend time with people and have good relations with them and be invested with them [...] Warren is not a good relative. If she were, she would have said, 'It's a priority that I meet with the Cherokee Nation and find out what I did wrong'[...] As scholars of race have shown, it is one of the privileges of whiteness to control everyone else's identity.[4]

---

4   Geoff McMaster, 'Indigenous DNA no proof of Indigenous identity, says Native studies scholar', University of Alberta, Folio, November 5th, 2018.

TallBear is very clear that there is no such thing as a DNA test that can 'prove' Indigenous ancestry, but that does not mean that DNA tests are totally useless, and many tribal councils do employ them. But it is only in the last few decades when that status has come to mean anything material. TallBear traces the rise of DNA testing to the 1970s and 80s in the United States when tribes started building bingo halls and casinos and bringing in significant revenues for their members. All of a sudden American Indians started showing up everywhere, claiming ancestry and wanting a piece of that pie.

In recent years, decolonial efforts have forced universities, governments and funding agencies to prioritize Indigenous hiring and support. Now, who is and who is not Indigenous matters in a very real, very material and very painful way. It is a zero-sum calculation in many cases: if a faux-Indigenous person gets a job or a grant, it means a person with legitimate Indigenous heritage and family does not. Playing Indian is not just an embarrassing affectation, it is stealing. Not just identity, but money and power. Tallbear speaks about that power in terms of political authority:

> I want to be careful with the argument that it's culture versus biology; it's also political authority versus biology. We have debates amongst ourselves about whether being Native American is about being a citizen of your tribe – a political designation – or about culture and traditional practice. I tend to come down on the side of political citizenship. It's true that it's about much more than blood – culture matters. But our political autonomy matters too, and that helps produce a space in which our cultural traditions can thrive.[5]

This is the route back to thinking about community. We remain curious and optimistic about the promise of a non-processual and especially non-teleological view of history, but let's not get precious about it. In the wake of ongoing colonial devastation, our ideas about community and

---

5   Linda Geddes, 'There is no DNA test to prove you're Native American' in New-Scientist, Feb 5, 2014.

togetherness have to remain constantly unfixed. Good relations should never be stable, but porosity in the service of erasure can never be abided by.

There are questions that remain: how can unfixity land down in everyday, non-anthropocentric ways of being in the world? How can it be that friendship – of claiming one another – surpasses borders – not metaphorically but physically? Is friendship actually a vehicle for resistance to nationalism and coloniality?

Interview with Leela Gandhi

Leela Gandhi is a post-colonial theorist based at Brown University and author of the book, *Affective Communities: Anti-Colonial Thought, Fin-de-siè-cle Radicalism and the Politics of Friendship* as well as other works including *Common Cause*. As we were working through this book, we were struck by how Leela navigated some of the key questions we kept getting stuck on, in particular, her ideas of 'unfinishedness', of the mobility of friendship as a figure for democracy and of friendship as perpetual affective motion. Her unwillingness to default to easy constraints and definitions opened a ton of theoretical territory for us.

AJ/MH: In a lot of our conversations with people, and in a lot of our thinking, we have found a definitional problem: what is friendship? There is a long historical twitch that threads through many different intellectual traditions trying to define friendship: what exactly is it, how can it be defined, how can it be categorized?

LG: I've been keenly interested in tracing and giving voice exactly to how (within a transcultural genealogy of the concept) friendship is the positive possibility rather than problem, as you put it, of something that cannot either be categorized or defined: yet which is unmistakable when you're in its vicinity. I've come to this understanding by degrees.

In my book, *Affective Communities*, on anticolonial thought and the politics of friendship, I started out with an interest in a non-antagonistic historiography for thinking about colonial encounters. My parameters were circumscribed by the geography and chronology of the South Asian-British/European colonial encounter at the last *fin de siècle*: a liminal moment before the emergence of the irremediably jingoistic, totalizing and instrumentalizing new imperialisms that started to emerge in the twentieth century; and which were countered by necessary but hardened forms of xenophobic cultural nationalisms. We are still heir to the formations engendered by these antagonisms on both sides: in the spheres of economy, ecology, aesthetics, knowledge, and so on.

Now, by antagonism (or antagonistic historiography) I don't just mean a situation where there are battlelines, factions, hostilities (sometimes we must take sides and identify with precise causes for precise ends). It is more about how in reified *hostilities of two*, let's call it (dialectical thinking included, as we know from Mikhail Bakhtin, the great thinker of dialogic forms) there is a desperate quest for *settlement* of this or that ethical and political truth or vantage. Anticolonial nationalisms are examples of this sort of settlement.

In early Indic ecumenical thought (Hindu, Muslim, Buddhist, Jain, and Indigenous belief systems, combined) there is a deep suspicion – a phobia even – of thinking by two. The medieval mystic-poet, Kabir, tells us that occurrences of two (in the matter of gender, religion, species, for example) bring on an anguish of settlement and clarification at any cost. He recommends the position of the *middle*, which is not a zone of neutrality but rather a locus where clarities, final shapes, and immutable forms (definitions and categories, no less) are *called into question* . There is no aversion here to forms as such – life after all is no more no less than forms of life (work, vacation, love, protest, communication). The problem occurs when our imagination and actions become inflexibly transitive, namely, attached to this or that object and objective: to that one and nothing else, selective, partial viewpoints, values, domains, and norms. *Kabir says, the one who stands in the middle crosses the ocean in an instant. The world of two extremes is drowning. Two is torment. The fire bird makes its nest in the sky. It remains in between, far from earth and sky* – and here's the striking envoi – *its confidence is not based on anything*.

When I was engaged in the inquiry just described, friendship seemed to me a powerful figure for something like Kabir's non-antagonism of the middle: a willful blurring of settlement projects on either side of any divide; and a suspension, however transitory, of formation, clarification, actualization. I was very interested, in historical terms, of westerners who became powerful critics of the imperial project, thereby giving up their own entitlements] to the considerable spoils and advantages of empire. Many of the radicals who created a *zone of uncertainty* in the heart of the imperial project (that's what I'm interested in, more than any story of crossing over to the other side) were actively engaged in friendships with colonized counterparts and interested in the ethical possibilities of friendship as above. So, for example, the homosexual reformer Edward Carpenter (read and admired by M.K. Gandhi), who believed quite whimsically and beautifully that gender normativity was at the crux of the imperial attitude, posited friendship as an intense yet non-binary anti-colonial relation: a relation in which there is no teleology toward reproductive economy, no future posterity, no social role allocation and so on. Yet, it is specific and singular, in the sense of friendship with x or y or between x and y, and so on.

AJ/MH: Since you've written *Affective Communities*, has your thinking changed about friendship and community? And you talk a little bit about these notions of border crossing solidarities that aren't fixed in advance. We're wondering how you're thinking about these things today?

LG: In my more recent work, a book called, *Common Cause*, I've explored the relational dimension of friendship as a project of *imperfection*: it can be explained in terms of the grammatical distinction between *imperfective* and *perfective* verbs. Imperfective verbs are temporally capacious. They include past, present, future tenses and describe incomplete and iterative activities. By contrast, perfective verbs (forms of settlement) are restricted to past and future activities, and express actions (projects, aspirations) that are fully and finally completed (or projected to be so). In these terms, friendship is available for uptake as a commitment to *making unfinished*.

In social terms, we know it is good to have friends (for mental health, psychological well-being), but it is ultimately something that is its own end, without final form outside itself. It does not give us any known social rewards (except in the cynical sense of friends in high places). It is dissociable from the property relations at the heart of the biological family. It is not something you can inherit – or if someone else's friendships (e.g., of your parents or siblings) fall to you, they must be cultivated anew to have any chance of surviving and flourishing in your own life. When we enter friendship, then, we could say we enter – perhaps, unknowingly, and unconsciously at first – into a category of love and affection, affect, *tout court* – that arises from the dissolution of instrumental social contract relations. Such friendship becomes ethical when we are mindful and appreciative of its disorientation.

I should add, there is an aspect and promise of friendship in all relations, even the most contractual and abstract (as with the state, for example, in our capacity as citizens). When we mine friendship qualities in any relationship, from the most ossified to the most incidental, we are engaged in intransitivity, imperfection: the work of making unfinished. In this guise, I've argued, friendship is a figure for *democracy*. This idea has been pursued by various contemporary theorists of friendship. It was certainly germane to the subcultures explored in *Affective Communities*. Edward Carpenter's most substantive thinking on friendship, for instance, occurs in a book called *Towards Democracy*.

In the western radical intellectual and critical-theoretical tradition, imperfectionist democracy (friendship-based democracy, to gather all the threads) is often rendered as a mode of *utopian inclusivity*, premised on keeping the gates open: to this or that institution, this or that privilege and obligation, indeed, to the future itself (which may include the end of utopian inclusivity). Derrida's model of hospitality is apposite here. I've been very moved by thinking along these lines. Of late, though, I'm interested in the emergence with respect to the points above, of another ideal of *renunciation* in political life, which summons but does not belong unqualified to some untrammeled non-western tradition. It arrives at the way we think now about revolution and radical democracy out of the entanglement (in the very early twentieth century) of the European human sciences and orientalism: it entails a complex appropriation (and resistances, responses to such appropriations) of non-western, specifically Indic, and Asian antiquities – in the service of global modernism. The conceit of renunciation, at this juncture, is not other-worldly and life-denying. Rather it indicates a kind of restlessness – perpetual motion – the better to make revolutionary or reformist politics perennial rather than permanent.

Is friendship perpetual affective motion? Perhaps the portion of friendship in all our relations is just so: mobile, kinetic, nomadic, constantly starting over again?

AJ/MH: We were wondering, do you think that friendship even has a political horizon worth pursuing? What about friendship with the more-than-human? What would you say about that?

LG: Yes, it is essential to imagine relations of friendship with the non-human: animals, certainly, but why not stones, and the air we breathe? Forests? Oceans? Gods and monsters? Why not dreams, in so far as dreams belong to another species of consciousness? In *Affective Communities* I was very absorbed with the notion of *xenophilia*: the consideration of friendship as a disposition towards strangers and whatever is or seems foreign and other to the subject of perception. Over time I've become less persuaded by the self/other model which has dominated ethical thinking in the wake of European phenomenology and post-structuralism. This model is far too wedded to the profound influence and adaptation in western philosophy of the notion of *entelechy*: the importance of each of us having distinct, discrete, and separate irreversible configuration; in the breach of which we allegedly interfere with each other's unique vital growth and potential.

There are models for relationality from other traditions, western and non-western, modern and ancient alike, that tell us something different: make yourself homologous (establish identity and likeness) with the dog, the bird, the ocean, the air. The recommendation bypasses anxieties about erasing the alterity of putative others. The focus is on relaxing our own *ipseity*, i.e., what we think of as our minimal irreducible selfhood, and to do so in the spirit of recreation. We have very appealing cues for this sort of exercise from some of the great culture crossing dramaturges and performance theorists of our time. The polish director Jerzy Grotowski, whose work profoundly draws on Asian performance traditions, for instance, suggests that in any act (or acting) of relation or dialogue we begin by making a gift of *our* own formation, *our* distinct identity-attachment, if only for the duration of a performance: *I am giving myself to you for safekeeping until the show ends.* To the animal interlocutor summoned by your question, we might say in this vein, *I am giving you custody of my putative species distinction for the duration of the performance of our friendship.*

I am very intrigued by what the figure of *performance* (and its duration) liberates; for friendship or of any vested action and thought. It brings aspects of play, provisionality, experimentation, carnival into the grave matters of *the* political and *the* ethical, and a certain liberation from the matter of core existential and ontological orientation. I mean who lives by means of core existential orientation all the time? We are always trying things out, rehearsing, remaking, revising our projects.

AJ/MH: We're wondering when we think about the climate emergency, what are the political possibilities of friendship – are there some new ways we might think about these entanglements?

LG: Ah that's a big question. I don't have easy answers; except to say that the desire to redress the crisis and think sincerely about coexistence certainly comes from a place of friendship.

7. Kith and Kin

Kith is an odd word, rolling off the tongue awkwardly. It only ever seems to show up attached to *kin*, but has a long lineage in English of at least a thousand years. At one point it meant 'knowledge of something', or the 'land you are from', but now has come to mean something close to 'friends' or everyone you are close to who is not a direct relative. It gestures toward a phrase we are interested in: good relationships, which might be a synonym for substantive concern for the other.

Kin is a word in much more common circulation, recognizable on the covers of hipster lifestyle magazines and TV shows revolving around the 'unbreakable bonds of blood and family' that are repeatedly broken. Kin evokes family primarily, but gestures to larger values of hearth-and-home, of simpler fidelities and wholesomeness. Certain environmental movements enthusiastically call for us to view the more-than-human as *kin* in the hope that if we see other forms of life as family, we will recognize them as being just like us, and thus we will be less likely to damage them.

Donna Haraway has famously written often about 'making kin' with other animals, notably in *When Species Meet* and *Staying with the Trouble*:

> Making kin seems to me the thing that we most need to be doing in a world that rips us apart from each other [...] By kin I mean those who have an enduring mutual, obligatory, non-optional, you-can't-just-

cast-that-away-when-it-gets-inconvenient, enduring relatedness that carries consequences.[1]

This sounds lovely of course, and Haraway is someone whose writing we admire very often, but narratives of kinship, when shaped by the hands of Western philosophical traditions, hazard something perilous: reenacting orderings that forge togetherness as an identity of like-recognizing-like. Recognizing or imagining another as kin, maybe especially across species might be a moving experience, but what about all the others who you do not recognize, who are incommensurably different, who you share little or nothing in common? Ordering relations based on kinship threatens to re-enact and fix the world in place. There is a reason that muscular national and imperial projects tell us that we have to protect the Motherland at all costs, or that citizens must give to everything for the Fatherland – they wrap us in suffocating and totalizing renditions of togetherness, kinship from which there is no escape and no argument.

Christina Sharpe starts her essay 'Lose Your Kin' citing Sadiya Hartman: "Slavery is the ghost in the machine of kinship." She then cites racist US Senators Hammond and Thurmond as a route to detailing how white kinship recognizes itself while refusing to acknowledge Black personhood, assigning non-whites the designation of property and concretizing the whiteness of kin as an ordering mechanism:

> Slavery is the ghost in the machine of kinship. Kinship relations structure the nation. Capitulation to their current configurations is the continued enfleshment of that ghost.

> Refuse reconciliation to ongoing brutality. Refuse to feast on the corpse of others. Rend the fabric of the kinship narrative. Imagine otherwise. Remake the world. Some of us have never had any other choice.[2]

---

1   Steve Paulson, 'Making Kin: An Interview with Donna Haraway, in LA Review of Books,' December 6th 2019.
2   Christina Sharpe, 'Lose Your Kin', The New Inquiry, November 16th, 2016.

The idea of seeing a stranger, or animal or lake and desiring the comfortable recognition, the enduring relatedness of kin is always attractive, but it carries with it the full weight of white supremacy and coloniality. There are probably routes to making 'kin' a decent vehicle for being-together, for blowing up the idea of family so thoroughly and insistently that it becomes permeable and malleable enough to remake the worlds around us. There might well be other traditions that can view kin in entirely different lights, when being related does not mean same-recognizing-same. But in settler and Western grammars, invoking kin risks far too much. If 'kinship relations structure the nation', why not imagine other routes to community?

As Judith Butler writes: "It is not possible to separate questions of kinship from property relations (and conceiving persons as property) and from the fictions of "bloodline," as well as the national and racial interests by which these lines are sustained."[3] When ecological movements insist on 'kinning' it sounds to our ears far too much like drawing the more-than-human into existing relations that structure the world-as-it-is. It sounds like closing the loop, making complete an ordering that sees some persons as recognizable and others as disposable property.

So what then of kith? We are not really even sure how that idea might be deployed, but it is appealing in its awkward unfamiliarity. It speaks to friendship, and to what Leela calls 'imperfect, inorganic relationships, something that has no final form, something you do not inherit – a commitment to making unfinished'. The commitment to unfinishing is particularly powerful. It thinks past the fixities of reciprocity or comradeship or other transactionalist modes of being together to something more imaginatively collaborative, a disordering that permits a universe of possible relations, of ways of being together that do not require repetitions of the world as it is.

**

3   Judith Butler, Is Kinship Always Already Heterosexual?, A Journal of Feminist Cultural Studies, 13.1 2002, p14.

One sparkling winter day we pulled into the parking lot of the Stein Valley Nlaka'pamux Heritage Park just outside of Lytton, BC, and weren't at all surprised to see no one else there. The park is gigantic – more than 1000 sq/km in total – with 150 km of hiking trails through a protected watershed that is of intense spiritual, cultural and material importance to the Nlaka'pamux people.

The park is not all that easy to get to. The Stein Valley was the site of some pitched battles in the 1980s and 90s over proposed logging, but the correct side won, and now the park is managed via the Stein Valley Co-operative Management Agreement between the Lytton First Nation and the Province of BC. To get there you have to drive a few hours north of Vancouver to the village of Lytton, cross the river on a little reaction ferry, then drive up a dirt road for 10km or so.

That road travels through Nlaka'pamux land scattered with occasional houses and small farms winding up to the park. Once you get to the entrance you drive a few kilometers in to the trailhead, and, should you be so inclined, it is ideal for some dusty-parking-lot-donuts in your rented vehicle.

That winter afternoon was especially calm and surprisingly warm. We had not seen any cars coming either way, had seen no one out in their yards or the road. The lot was deserted, quiet enough to hear the river pounding down below and the wind rustling the pine trees. As we were packing up for a day-hike, a giant, rough-looking dog came gently trotting up the road. He was in no hurry, but aimed straight for us. We were momentarily on guard, wondering if he was coming to defend his territory, but we relaxed almost immediately: this guy clearly had no malice in his mind. He strolled over for a quick head-scratch, then did his rounds, sniffing the truck, pissing on stuff, criss-crossing the lot seeing who had been through lately. We watched him for a minute, figured he must be from one of the nearby farms, then loaded up our packs and started down the trail.

Charmingly, the dog joined us. He was a powerfully-built, thick beast. Probably 140 pounds, with a rough white coat that was dirty and full of brambles, but he was still startlingly handsome. He joined us just like any companion, walking with us on the trail, occasionally stopping or running ahead to do his own thing, but basically just joining in. We hiked for a couple of hours in one direction, mostly tracing the river, but periodically dipping into the forest, or traversing a bluff. The park was as spectacular as everyone says, with no one around at all, except our new dog friend.

When we stopped for a rest, our companion wandered around the river's edge, drinking out of little pools here and there, then came and flopped down beside us. We shared our snack with him: he was definitely interested in the salmon jerky, but not overly so. He liked the almonds and the granola bar too, but didn't seem all that hungry, and definitely was not begging. This dog had a wholly unfamiliar vibe – he wasn't obsequious or clingy or desperate for attention/approval/food. He wasn't really any of the typical dog-things. He was just there, hanging out. After a while we turned around and retraced our steps back to the car with our companion strolling along peacefully. The whole time we could barely contain our delight.

When we got to the vehicle, we weren't really sure how to proceed. We opened the trunk of the car to see if he wanted a ride somewhere, but he sneered at that. After some fussing around we decided to just leave. As we drove out, the dog ran behind, beside and in front of the car, happily marking us. At some point, maybe a mile or two out, he just peeled off without a word and jogged into the bush.

We were captivated. We talked about it for days after, always wondering what the dog was thinking: was he protecting us from bears? Was he a guide? Did he just want someone to go for a walk with? The experience continues to baffle us and confound easy analysis – it was a wholly singular kind of relationship for us, one not really repeated before or since. The only thing we sort of settled on is that he felt like a friend, like he had happily agreed to a relationship without bribe or threat, obligation or transaction.

We have no conceptual apparatus or names easily available to describe that experience, and we mourn that lack while celebrating what the absence makes available. How can we think of that absence as something other than poverty? Can we simultaneously name and not name that as friendship?

When Leela says friendship is a commitment to being unfinished "which is not to say that friendship is in itself undefinable or friendship is in itself something vague" that opens up the terrain for us. We mostly know how to interact with animals. There is a pretty standard palette of human/animal relationships available to most humans. We hunt, fear, goggle at wild animals. Breed, nurture, raise, eat, stare at captives. Care for, obsess and dote on pets. When an animal does not adhere to those categories it reorders our commitments and maybe offers something of a horizon. If we can stay there and let our animal relationships – as much as our relationships with humans and the rest of the more-than-human world stay unfinished, to 'think the absence of the name as something other than a privation', to let our relations be incomplete, then maybe that opens up ways that remake being-together.

8. Anyone Who Likes Cats and Dogs Is a Fool

Asking whether humans can be friends with animals is fraught. So many people have such intense relationships with animals, perhaps most especially their pets, that hazarding that question is affectively perilous and something of a philosophical watershed. Tread lightly, or inevitably someone who is BFFs with their budgie will cancel you for your callousness.

When Deleuze and Guattari dropped "Anyone who likes cats and dogs is a fool" and then returned and developed the argument recursively throughout *A Thousand Plateaus*, they were in part trying to argue that owning a pet distances and bulwarks humans from their own animality. They were longing to relate to a cat as animal-to-animal, not as human-to-animal, and in the process recover something of their own animality.

There are many salient points of critique of the Deleuze-Guattari desire for becoming-animal, depths that Donna Harraway has famously plumbed. Among them is the strangeness of claiming that a pet is an animal, when they have so patently entered into a different, hybrid, maybe becoming-human zone. The question for us here is whether friendship is a mode of relationship that offers any interspecies traction: or, can we be friends with *any* more-than-humans? And if so, how would we know?

The proposition that humans and more-than-humans might relate to one another as friends rests on acknowledging that pets, animals, plants, rivers, mountains and all the rest have active subjectivities, and might be willing to consider an offer of friendship. We suggest that all of us, human and more-than, are constantly shaping and reshaping our lives and histories, we all have beliefs and values and opinions of our own, and are enigmatic, surprising and capricious, within species as much as between.

For many of us, the easiest route to considering animal subjectivities is to talk to our pets and wonder about the ways we spend time together. Thinking about pets is to think about captivity and property and ownership, but also to consider how pets keep and care for us, often as much as the reverse. Some pets may well be fundamentally satisfied, even delighted with the safety, comfort and companionship their relationship status affords, but being held pet-captive also comes with very obvious losses: of freedom, adventure and other-animal interactions for both sides of the relationship. For all pets as much as humans, parsing those gains and lacks is a complex calculus to be constantly considered and evaluated.

Domestication and captivity come in many shifting shapes and guises. Expansionist human domination has left us managing the lives of animals near and far – from those we raise to kill and eat, to 'wild' animals that we feed off our back porches, to pets that sleep in our beds, to those whose habitats we maintain and protect – but fixed categorical indexing of these relationship deprives animals of their own creativities and striving.

Which of us – of any species anywhere – are not constantly making compromises to maintain certain relationships? Which of us enters into completely voluntary, consensual, or mutualistic encounters with anyone else, without any impositions on our decision-making? It is a consumptive fantasia of unfettered 'choice' to imagine that any of our lives are like shoe-shopping on the internet with a seemingly endless array of possible options. We are always constrained and impelled, and thankfully so. Animals of all kinds are constantly making choices – individually and collectively – based on new and old and incomplete information.

Who knows for certain what any animal is thinking? Who knows whether any more-than-human is happy, or satisfied, or frustrated, or their ambitions being savagely thwarted? We can make our best guesses and labour to communicate – just like we do with any other humans – but ultimately have to defer to their incommensurability.

Being-together really does rest on *whateverness*: loving your pet cats includes rubbing their stomach just as much as that gross playful live-dismembering thing they do with the mice they catch, just as much as acknowledging all the ineffable practises and worldviews of every more-than-human entity. Becoming-friends does not rely on 'our' animality, or 'their' becoming-humanness, it rests on the willingness to acknowledge each other's subjectivity far beyond the carceralized renditions of categorical identity, including *species*.

Politics are not, and cannot, be just between humans. With pets, animals we eat, captured and 'wild' animals, the possibility of friend-relationships is always there and thus the possibility of politics. To insist on kinship is to occlude that possibility – to collapse that relationship into relatedness or likeness – or, in Nancy's words, it then "necessarily loses the *in* of being-*in*-common. Or, it loses the *with* or the *together* that defines its essence. It yields its being-together to a being *of* togetherness." As Martha Nussbaum puts it:

> This quality of active, striving agency suggests that animals are not only objects of wonder but also subjects of justice [...] Wonder suggests that animals matter directly, for their own sake – not because of some similarity they have to ourselves [...] animals matter because of what *they* are, not because of kinship to ourselves.[1]

The impossibility of surety in any of our more-than-human relationships defines the field of unfixity, of being unfinished. Do any animals feel 'substantive concern' for us? Does a river have any care for human experience? Could a tree agree to being in relationship with us? Maybe. If so, how would we know? Those questions are burdened by the limits of language and (most of) our human imagination. But if humans can acknowledge the creativity and subjectivity of every more-than-human entity, recognize the own-ness, the flat-ontological existence of both species and individual, their own ineffabilities, that is to open up the

---

1   Martha Nussbaum, *Justice for Animals*, New York: Simon and Schuster, 67, 2023.

chance of a politics marked by negotiation, compromise, fluidity and porousnesss.

Animals and other beings are not metaphors. The desire to use the more-than-human world as justification in-of-itself for prescribing human relationships is one more rhetorical ploy. Free-market enthusiasts have long deployed Darwin as the validation for a world driven by competition, survival of the fittest, and 'natural' hierarchies. Those of us interested in socialist socialities cite Kropotkin's rendition of evolution as full of mutual aid, cooperation and reciprocity. Certain naturalists see forms of symbiosis in the more-than-human world as the template for human social organization. It's all fine and good to notice admirable relational practises anywhere and go about building aspirational politics around them. But reducing animals or rivers of trees to theatrical props is just bad manners and does damage to our capacity to be in relationship.

Any ethological (or ontological) efforts that deny or collapse the striving and creativity of animals and more-than-humans is just barking up the wrong tree, but respectful inquisitiveness is another thing altogether. Belgian philosopher Vinciane Despret's book *Living as a Bird* strikes us as an example of a generous curiosity. Starting with close observations of the warbling blackbird, she asks why so many birds emerge from long winter's migrations and generally peaceful co-existence and then seemingly all of a sudden start singing and acting aggressively, defending territory and brawling with other birds.

Despret argues that birds have very different conceptions of 'home' and 'space' than most humans tend to. It's hard to claim that birds 'live in' or 'inhabit' one place: their relationships to space are just so different from ours and they occupy a whole different set of dimensions. While we are stuck on the ground, birds move up and through vertical space in immeasurably shifting vectors and lines of flight, which as Despret notes, inflects everything, including their experiences of barometric fluctuations and atmospheric flows.

This multi-dimensional movement of birds through space cannot be reconciled with what she calls 'petit-bourgeois' renditions of territory and private property that have traditionally marked ornithological explanations for bird behaviours. Birds appear to be aggressively defending territory, but not in the propertarian sense of seizing public land for individual ownership and then defending its borders against incursion. Her observations suggest that there are zones of spatial contestation, peripheries of occupation where skirmishes flare up, and then dissipate into 'nothing personal', just regular reorganizations of who gets to hang out where.

Ethologists, burdened by their extant assumptions of private property, have habitually observed animals and then let those jaundiced eyes travel into human social prescriptions for territorial allocations with the supposed evidence of property as 'natural'. Despret says that for birds, territory only exists in the making of it, and that there are no fixed lines or borders to their territoriality, there are only malleable zones of social possibility, interactions and re-positioning.

Does this mean that Despret's study of birds, or any other evidence of non-sovereign, non-propertarian territoriality among animals is justification for our own arguments towards a borderless world? That'd be very handy, but sadly no. There is a universe of different kinds of birds and even among very specific flocks of very specific species, there is still a world of difference. Birds are themselves; they are just like every other person. We love the idea of porous territorial zones that open whole realms of new socialities, but not because it is a 'natural' construct. We might admire and wonder about certain modes of life, and suggest they are worthy of emulation, but not as some kind of teleological historical task.

Birds are birds, they are not metaphors. They are full of mystery and weirdness and incompletenesses. It is only in that incommensurableness that politics becomes possible. We had no idea what that dog in the Nlaka'pamux Heritage Park was up to – was it going to attack us, was it just a little curious, was it bored, was it looking for companionship, did it just feel like going for a walk, was it worried about bears taking us out? All of those, none of those? Or maybe all those human-described human motivations expressed in our slender human languages are just inadequate for even approximating the range and mystery of that dog's thinking and feeling. It's always fun to speculate and laugh about what that dog had in mind, but ultimately the only available thing is to enjoy and marvel in its company.

Those zones of unsurety, of unfixity, are precisely the political. That dog was not an enemy, even if it attacked on sight. But neither was it kin – that was not *like meeting like*. The dog was not attempting to animalize us, nor we humanize it. We have no conceptual apparatus or names easily available to describe that experience, except maybe *friend*.

The specific cringiness of someone calling themselves the 'mom' or 'dad' of their pets – or worse, talking about their 'fur babies' (!) – is augmented by its gesture towards a comfortable desire for human superiority, positioning pets as being kept and protected by benevolent guardians. It relegates that relationship back to familiar and bounded forms, ones that centre humans as the titular heads and progenitors of the 'family'. Charming interspecies interactions are a cause of constant joy – as much as in real life as on the internet – specifically because they upend expected fidelities. Dogs cuddling with pigs, cats grooming monkeys, capybaras chilling with everyone: any kind of unusual combination is a delight, as much as when a bird is willing to eat seeds out of your hand or a seal swims along beside your canoe.

The unfamiliarity of interspecies relationships is the experience of exposure, of not knowing exactly how to behave or what to expect, not being able to defer to familiar reflexes. Leaving easy relational confines, especially across species, requires a different kind of attentiveness, a gentleness, an observational presence, but also the constant possibility of loss. If being with a friend is always to grieve their coming loss, the becoming-grief of losing pets is telescoped because they die so young, or sometimes just leave capriciously. To love an animal is to be exposed to an often-way-too-soon loss, and often for reasons we cannot understand.

Suffering is endured alone but the particular kinds of tactility we have with the animals we keep – picking them up, feeding them, cuddling, caring for their injuries and maladies, helping them birth, eating them – exposes us to uncertain, unsure futures. It forces us to confront questions of domesticity and freedom, and of the ethics of our management of their lives and deaths, and suffering, the mass-scaled carcerality of animals that haunts modernity.

In a strange, pandemic-fueled sermon to open 2022, Pope Francis veered vertiginously off-script and claimed that keeping pets is "a denial of fatherhood and motherhood and diminishes us, takes away our humanity." He called it a "phenomenon of cultural degradation" and that when so many people choose keeping pets over having children, "we lose the richness of fatherhood and motherhood, and it is the country that suffers."[2] This polemic was exceedingly odd coming from a childless octogenarian who heads an organization famous for its brutality and endemic sexual abuse of children. It also raised the immediate fury of pet owners – Catholic and otherwise – across the globe. But perhaps he was on to something.

Being in relationship with animals *does* diminish us, in badly needed ways. To acknowledge the subjectivities of animals is to acknowledge the poverty of placing humans at the pinnacle of evolution, and to be willing to attend to uncertain, unfixed relationships. To be exposed to the suffering of animals and to be willing to confront the suffering of our pets can inflect our relations with other animals and more-than-human beings.

If Francis is concerned about the fate of 'the country' under assault from pet-owners, perhaps he was gesturing towards a possible unraveling of the colonial state and anthropomorphic dominations (maybe [...]?). Acknowledging the fluid and porous borders between human and animal, between living and non-living, between conscious and not, primes us for the possibilities of other kinds of borderlessness. The experience of unsurety that marks all our relationships with animals, and with friends, is precisely the flattened unfixity that makes borderlessness thinkable.

---

2   Harriet Sherwood, 'Choosing pets over babies is 'selfish and diminishes us', says pope', The Guardian, January 5th, 2022.

9. On Gentleness

Anne Dufourmantelle has written that crucial moments of our lives, particularly at the beginning and end, are marked by gentleness: the capacity to attend closely to another. The particular kind of attentiveness that gentleness demands is the terrain of exposure, an exposure given permission, made believable by touch.

Evoking gentleness carries real hazards. Being *gentle* can suggest a cloying anti-conflictual softness, a genteel gentility, a performatively tender underbelly, a bourgeois lack of grit. We want to suggest something else here: that gentleness is an unworking, a commitment and substantive care for the other.

Gentleness can move beyond appeasement to a site of agency, resistance and reflection as a mode of living, as a means to traverse anxieties, to not look away, and a vigilance to watch, patiently or not, and demarcate the contours of antagonism. Gentleness displayed at an unexpected, unanticipated moment has the power to overwrite, recode and produce new grammars of exchange. The good life corresponds to the possibility of being together, in a politics that has a horizon beyond the human and a capacity to attend to an entwined exposure. It is not a retreat or an escape or simply a place of symbolic resistance. In and of itself, it has the power to reorder our relations with one another and the more-than-human. To act gently is a form of power that is a real force of resistance.

Gentleness is often presented as the opposite of brutality and vulgarity, as the sweetness of living, a place to recover time. If we wanted to imagine a borderless world, something beyond the dreams of a state or a nation or an ethnicity, the agility to think around traditional demarcation lines allows a way into that possibility. In the material life of the everyday, in the very risk of living, in the porosity of touching, we can sense the possibility of a new kind of relation and politics through exposure to one another and the more-than-human.

Our relationships with animals, especially pets, are often marked by a startling gentleness. Companion animals instigate all kinds of behaviours, from creepy baby-talk to absurd authoritarianisms and violence, but maybe more than anything, human-animal interspecies relationships are marked by touching. If we are even half-sure an animal won't attack or bite, our instincts impel us to reach out, to invite the bird to eat out of our hands, to stroke the neighbour's cat, to invite the roadside bear to sniff the car window, to blow in a horse's nose, to touch the horn of a passing cow.

Our instincts with animals are often stupid and dangerous and regrettable but speak to a shamelessness that the desire to touch evokes. We know that whale-watching and zoos and aquariums are brutal, demeaning exercises, imprisoning or harassing animals for our own amusement, but they also give permission to delight. The argument that the suffering of specific animals in captivity is justified by the generalised empathy seeing them evokes for the rest of the more-than-human world is an awful apologism, a trade we should never agree to, but there is truth there.

Being in proximity to animals we would never encounter otherwise dislodges our own gentleness, partially because of their size and shape and capacities, but also because we have no permission to touch. With pets we are afforded a passport to tactility, to physical points of corporeal exchange where there is simultaneous recognition of strange incommensurabilities and of permeable borders.

The feeling of a cat licking your arm, a dog resting its head on your lap, or a bird sitting on your shoulder instigates a kind of timelessness, a suspension of belief, and a relief that temporary passage has been granted. The flesh on fleshness of touching an animal is also always a risk. There is always an unsettledness, an unsurety that the animal won't bite or claw or scare you for unclear reasons, even animals you have touched a thousand times before. Touching an animal requires an attentiveness, a presence, an alertness, a demand to be right there, right now, otherwise you might get bit or stomped or clawed. It is a presence that recognizes an animal's particular subjectivity, its own-ness to itself.

This attentiveness is redolent of the quiet dance before you go in for a hug with a stranger, that moment when you try to figure out if the person you are meeting wants a kiss on the cheek or on both cheeks, a high five, a fist bump, a handshake, hand on your heart, or just a smile. Touching, or not, with a stranger or across species, in that moment of attentiveness is something of gentleness.

Tactility, in touching another body, maybe especially animal bodies, does a welcome trick in undermining contemporary fetishizations of ontological alterities. In having to be present, to be alert to unexpected reactions in suspended fleshly borderlessness, requires that we shed most of our generalized beliefs about how 'dogs' act, or what 'birds' like, or how 'cows' want to be touched.

Broad indexing of animal behaviour might be an initial point of departure, but every animal is its own, with its own opinions, preferences, and styles, just like the rest of us. Every bird – whether it is a crow on the porch, a cockatoo in a cage, or a starling in a murmuration- is full of its ownness. Touching, or not, asks for both a timely and a timeless attentiveness, a gentleness in learning how any one bird, or person, would be willing to touch or be touched, if at all.

Most of the urban Global North has hygienically cleansed its relationships with animals as much as with other humans. Our citified animal interactions are reduced to pet-companions, occasional incursions of raccoons or rats or birds, and steady maintenance and distance from most anything else. In much of the rural, working-class North and even more so across the Global South, human-animal interspecies relationships are more fulsome and co-habitational, learning from one another's presence – cows on the street, wet markets, strays everywhere, coyotes in the backyard, unwelcome insects getting into the house, macaques stealing food, sheep free-ranging.

Many of those encounters are tangential and everyday obstacles, but many of them are working relationships, labouring with and beside animals in what Radhika Govindrajan calls 'animal intimacies,' relationships that straddle "incommensurable differences" and "ineffable affinity."[1] They can be sweet and mutually beneficial, and also infused with power, control, confinement, and violence. Govindrajan writes of cows weaponized by Hindutva, women sexualizing bears, pigs who are sort of domesticated, monkeys as agents of enclosure – all kinds of dissonances and resonances, subtle and symbolic accommodations, constant negotiations that she calls interspecies relatedness – living and dying with animals around.

Animals are always leaking through our best plans: mice and ants and insects sneaking into the house past every defense, goats and sheep and cattle escaping through broken fences, cat and dogs running off, elephants stomping through villages and fields, raccoons destroying lawns, birds shitting all over your car. Learning to live with animals requires forms of exposure and gentleness sometimes over duration, sometimes very momentary.

The gentleness we are after here is an attentiveness, to animals as species but as individuals as well. Not a sycophantic willingness to appease them no matter what, nor a reflexive containment, extermination or driving off. Interspecies relations ask for a curious attention that can operate at multiple scales, individually and collectively.

Conventional renditions of gentleness tend to revolve around the withholding of possible violence or force, refusing domination or the shepherding of strength. The gentleness implied when holding a small animal is that if you are not careful, you could damage this sweet thing. If you are not attentive to how you hold a newborn you could hurt their neck. If you are visiting with someone going through a tough time you need to be careful with your words as they might be feeling particularly tender. This is a kind of gentleness that presumes weakness of the other, a gentleness willing to be exposed in its strength.

A more politically generative interspecies gentleness is an attentiveness that does not need to reduce the other, does not need to extract anything. As Oxana Timofeeva puts it, it is to think the sovereign beyond the

1   Radhika Govindrajan, Animal Intimacies, Chicago: University of Chicago Press, 2018.

human. The pleasure of touching fur or trunk or horn or claw or wing is delightful, but also unsteadying in its strange, tactile confirmation of the unbelievable things animals can do and are, things that humans are incapable of:

> By accepting our animality, I do not mean going back to nature, being natural, listening to one's nature – nothing of this kind. It is not about yoga, biological products, sexual freedoms, sports, and other more or less commercialized practices of self-care performed by contemporary bourgeois individuals. By accepting the animal that I am, I mean a movement toward self-alteration or dis-identifying that implies separating from the position of power. [...]. The attempt to go beyond individuality, to use my humanness merely as a point of departure or a bearer of the other, is not safe, as it breaks my autonomy, but this might be the way to the sovereign being beyond the human. The animal is already here, typing these letters, but to set it free requires a lot of theoretical and practical work that cannot be done in solitude: for this, a collective of various creatures is needed. How to create this collective and how to be a part of it – this is the question for the future interspecies politics.[2]

We submit that gentleness can be precisely this practical point of departure: an attentiveness and presence that hazards exposure. We know what this feels like, literally. It is a presence that might be called consent, a noticing that does not imply domination, nor weakness. It is a mode that the pandemic required of us constantly, noticing each other's comfort levels, masks on or off, inside or out, distanced or not. The proliferation of the virus, the porousness of where one's body begins and the other ends, and the matrices of entanglement, control, symptoms, shame, and the bodily chains of transmission that inextricably bind one to the other come to the surface where gentleness emerges as a site of daily political agency.

---

2   M. Buna, 'Why Still Look at Animals: A Conversation with Oxana Timofeeva', LA Review of Books, October 27th, 2018.

The same kinds of corporeal attentiveness are always in motion in playfulness. Playing is definitionally useless, it is extra, surplus behaviour. Playful fun is not required for survival, it overflows everyday drudgery, it has no material purpose, it is extravagant in its waste of time and energy. But to play well requires a very specific kind of attentiveness.

If you are playing pickup basketball you need to fit in to the intensity, skill level, fitness and style of everyone else in the game – if you do not or cannot notice, the game is compromised. In the midst of play-fighting, between animals and/or humans, participants have to modulate themselves even more closely. If someone plays too hard, and bites or wrestles or hits too aggressively, then the game is no longer fun, it's too much like actual fighting and someone likely gets hurt. If your play-fighting is lackluster, the game is no fun either, there's no energy, no thrill. If it does not approximate the adrenaline of fighting, the game is boring.[3]

It is always complicated to discern this goldilocks zone: what is just enough and not too much. It requires a close attentiveness to whoever you are play-fighting with, making sure they are not hurt, they are enjoying the experience, that they are not angry or frustrated. The right zone of play is never fixed, it is always moving, the borders are constantly being reset, and playfighters, whether wolf cubs or teenagers, have to be constantly alert to how their opponent is doing and feeling. It is a skill that most parents start teaching their offspring almost immediately. A mother dog moves from play to admonishment seamlessly if one of her offspring bites too hard: gently and powerfully grabbing her pup's neck with her jaw.

This gentleness is a critical feature of all sports, and especially combat and physical sports, where bodily damage is always at risk. The gentleness required to play these sports surprises people who are unfamiliar with boxing or jiu jitsu or football, games that are based around hitting or manipulating each other's bodies powerfully. To play these sports

---

3   Brian Massumi in What Animals Teach Us About Politics, Duke University Press, 2014 does a brilliant job thinking about animal play, we've just riffed on it here.

is always to be at real, very prescient risk and you can only enter knowing that your opponents have agreed to very specific conditions that will limit the amount of damage you incur. The zones of agreement are malleable and obscured, especially when players are tired or emotional, but are always central to the game's validity. When they are violated, deliberately or accidentally, it is an occasion of real concern. The gentleness that combatants or opponents feel for one another is visible after the game is over – players hugging, fighters tenderly confirming each other's welfare, players making sure they have not crossed too far over the lines.

Attentiveness is similarly required for verbal playfulness: teasing, poking, talking shit, sharing inside jokes, or ribbing each other. Friendly exposure suggests a willingness to have your own pomposities punctured, to have your dignity laughed at, to have our embarrassing stories surfaced. Our friends know what they can tease us about and when it's too much. Playfulness lets us drop our guards and relax, allows for an openness, but only if does not go too far. The lines are always shifting, some days we are happy to be teased other times are not up for it at all. Our friends are attuned to our modes, and we trust that they will care for us and not do actual damage, nor exploit our exposure.

Playfulness is a critical political mode: a gentle testing of the waters, setting and resetting limits, pushing and withdrawing. It is a creative act of borderlessness – with animals, between other animals, between humans. There is a mobilising role for playfulnesses we hazard and in determining the inside and outside. Gentleness isn't necessarily a natural or resting state of the world, but even when friends spar or play, there is a duty of attentiveness with one another. There is no friendship without a possible wound. The potential suffering, sacrifice and labour involved in friendship requires maintenance and malleability.

To imagine a being-with the more-than-human is to move gently into the open and reconsider what the preservation of human and more-than-human life entails. Exposure, playfulness, vulnerability, forgiveness, gentleness as a mode-of-life, in a political sense, suggests an ecological validity to move beyond the straitjacket of a closed, anthropocentric orientation.

Interview with Leanne Betasamosake Simpson

Leanne is a Michi Saagiig Nishnaabeg independent scholar, writer, musician, artist and friend. Leanne's many books including *As We Have Always Done* have been tremendously influential in grounding Indigenous approaches to social, political and ecological questions. We were both interested in talking to her about her own ideas about friendship and community, and as always, curious about how her thinking challenges ours. She has historically picked our arguments apart and pushed us hard in gentle and generous directions.

AJ/MH: This project started with us just meeting once a week in a bar to read and talk together. At the beginning we were just trying to think through and past racial nationalisms and xenophobias that are circulating in so many ways in the present ecological moment. Then we began to talk and wonder about friendship and community, and what they might have to say?

LBS: This practice of study really resonates with me. I'm drawn to the idea that our present moment requires getting together once a week, reading books, thinking together, thinking through together, not necessarily as a debate but towards understandings that are forged in relation to each other. Friendship as an intellectual and political practice has historically been quite important in Black feminist organizing and in Indigenous feminisms as well. In my experience, it isn't often "debate" or at least its thinking that takes place outside of the heteropatriarchy of the western academy and their practice of debate. I think about that all a lot in my work –the conversations around fires or kitchen tables, on the picket line, on the front step or in the park, at shows or protests that transform the way I think. These are almost always associated with some sort of collective action, whether that's a land based practice, or organization or making sure everyone in the community or the classroom has what they need to be able to contribute. For Indigenous peoples, this is the sort of study that is the fabric of our politics. Learning to voice when we disagree, to work through conflict in a way that is gentle and respectful, to sit with unpleasant emotions and then make decisions with integrity are very important communal practices in our politics.

There's often joy, and laughter and care in these spaces. Food. Ceremony. Joking around. Games. Because there's joy in all that and in relational politics building, maintaining and transforming relationships is the political work. For those of us who work out of the margins of the academy, whose work is informed by a struggle and movement building, I think that the methodology of thinking through with friends, thinking alongside friends, and having those real world relationships that are ongoing is a really important intervention into how knowledge is generated and shared. This is also important to do in community, with people you may or may not be friends with. It is important to do this across movements and sites of struggle as a practice of solidarity.

AJ/MH: We poked around the idea of kinning – the attempt to see the other-than-human as family. Maybe that sounds great if you belong to something or you know if you're kin with them, but what if you're not, what if you don't belong somewhere and how so easily distorted notions of community flow into notions of nationhood and belonging in the service of exposure.

LBS: If you are alive or were recently alive on planet earth, then you are part of a deep network of relationships that exist outside of your own body and sphere of influence. You belong.

I don't see the division between human and other-than-human, or human and non-human. I see a division between living and nonliving things, and even that is a bit fluid if you think along with sphagnum moss for instance, where only one cell in twenty is alive, but even the dead cells contribute to the structure. This idea of living and non-living though is reflected in and encoded in Nishnaabemowin, and the structure of our language, which is mostly verbs. And the way that you conjugate those verbs is based on whether things are animate or inanimate. And so that tells me that if you're looking at being in deep relationality with living things, you're thinking on a planetary scale, an intimate scale, a family scale, and a community scale. And that means that everything that is alive has spirit, and is also interacting in another realm. To me this represents a kind of humility that maybe we just don't know everything. There are other forces at work that we don't understand. So belonging isn't about the nation state. It's not a border, it's not a chunk of land with an army around it. It something more profound than that.

Biidaaban is a word in my language that means dawn. It means that first light, peeking over the horizon, before the sun has come up. It's composed of three smaller words. And in Nishnaabemowin, when you split the bigger word into the three tiny words, that's when the poetry and the theory actually spill out. The 'bii' part means the future is coming at you. The 'daa' is the present or home and 'ban' or 'ban' is a suffix that you would put on to the end of someone else's name when they passed on. So it denotes the past – so Biidaaban the present, which is the collapsing in of the future and the past. And so that, to me, is a really mind-blowing sort of concept in terms of thinking about how important the present is.

In Nishnaabeg thought, it is the present that gives birth to the future. This is when you plant the seeds. This is where this is where you can change the trajectory of the future. It places that kind of responsibility in the now. And I love that sort of reminder that you get every morning when the sun comes up about the importance of that presence and the importance of being alive and taking on that responsibility.

If you take that concept and add it to this deep relationality, then you've got ancestors, and you've got those yet to be born. You have a cosmos that is very much alive, that is multi-dimensional, and is made up of layers of relationships that are networked together. That's what I mean in my work, when I'm talking about this complex web of relationships between living things. The spectrum of relationships that I can have with plants and animals and spirits are the same spectrum of relationships that I can have with humans.

I'm interested in how we communally take on these responsibilities to live together in a way that brings forth more life. I have a responsibility to that web and to that set of interconnections and interdependencies to live in a certain way. And the way that I'm supposed to live in a way that promotes continuous rebirth that promotes a diversity of life and living, both on an intimate and on a planetary scale.

My ancestors were living in a way where they were practicing consent and accountability long before there was conflict. They were committed collectively to ethical practices that were based on systems of care, for the land and waters, for plants and animals and for societies that were different than their own. Individuals had a high degree of self-determination in order to be their best selves and to contribute to society. They treated other living things in particular ways to show respect. There are rituals and ceremonies that are done to make sure the animals we harvest feel respected even in death. We have stories of people marrying beavers and living intimately with beaver society for instance.

The practice of consent is really at the core of all those relationships, because people are constantly communicating with plants and animals and ancestors and those yet to be born, and constantly through embodied practice. Before we harvest a moose, we might place an offering and ask the moose to give itself up in the physical world so that we can feed our families. We would commit to using all the parts of the moose, taking only what we need, and sharing with other animals and people in our community.

I think that respect for the autonomy of other living things is a way of thinking about commune. It is a way of thinking with other forms of life. It is a way of taking care and to me, that is a very, very different way of making and living in a world.

AJ/MH: We've spoken to two scholars, Leela Gandhi and Julietta Singh – and both of them have cautioned us about trying to define the idea of friendship. As soon as you try to define it, it begins to lose its power. Julietta has this cool phrase where she says, it's the relationships that we don't have a name for. Friendship is what's left after we have named and fixed all the other relationships. And we like that a lot, but sometimes we get stuck, it's a conceptual hang-up for us, like if we're going to talk about something, we have to know what we're talking about. Do we need to put some guardrails on the conversation in your opinion or is friendship something that we cannot, should not define?

LBS: In English, friend is used to refer to a spectrum of relationships and of intimacies. If I'm friends with someone, there is an element of care involved. In Nishnaabemowin, and in the ethical framing I'm talking about, there is a series of ethical practices that one engages in whether or not the other living being is a friend. Consent, non-interference, accountability, respect for individual self-determination, building consensus, repairing and transforming harm. All of that must happened whether or not I think of the other living being as a friend or not.

   In Nishnaabemowin, one of our words for the being that made the world is Gzhwe Manidoo. It means the one who loves us most completely, the one who loves our naked selves, the one who loves unconditionally. I think about the practice of unconditional love and how it was an instigator in the making of this world. It is a reminder that living things have the capacity to live within mino-bimaadiziwin, or continuous rebirth, and also the capacity to destroy life. And when forces are out to destroy life, then to me at least, our responsibilities become quite clear. This is why Indigenous peoples put their bodies on the lines to protect lands and waters from pipelines and mining and deforestation. This is why water protectors are protecting springs and headwaters. This practice of care isn't based on friendship, it's based on a belief that the water inside our bodies is related to water cycling through the planet, and all living things share that water.

AJ/MH: We want to cycle back for a second to ask you about this idea of borderlessness. We've been thinking about borderlessness in the wake of racial nationalisms and policing and surveillance states. The idea of borderlessness is very attractive in lots of ways, but Indigenous Nations and other kinds of threatened communities often require protecting sovereign borders and asserting nationhood.

LBS: It's hard to mark the Anishinaabe on a map because our "borders" were pretty leaky. There is a part of the world, around the Great Lakes where we have a strong presence, where we governed ourselves through embodied politics and deep relationality. I live in the eastern part of that formation. There are places close to where I live where our origin stories take places. We always shared time and space with other living things. We share land, water and air with billions of other living things that are intimately connected to all forms of life on the earth. Humans have a responsibility to live within the living networks we're a part of. I think of the bush or the forest of a gathering place of many different species and forms of life. I think of the tall grass prairie as a gathering place of many different species and forms of life. The Black Oak Savanna is in between and there is a spectrum of many different communities as you move between these open ecological systems. There is distinction, but there is no border.

We were never the "only human ones" in our homeland. Michi Saagiig Nishnaabeg homeland is an eco-tone, the overlapping of two eco zones that creates a place of incredible diversity. The Wendat (Huron) often lived amongst us living in longhouses and farming. To the south, our presence gradually decreases. Nishaabeg place names become fewer and Haudenosaunee places names become greater. In these zones we had more intensive diplomacy. We spent more time working out our differences, negotiating ways of living peacefully. These overlapping lands, shared spaces weren't unique in my way of thinking. We were already sharing land and water with beavers and moose and ducks and fish. We were already forming ecosystems that were connected to other ecosystem. There was already an intimate practice of internationalism. Embodied politics is a constant cycle of accountability, consent and communication.

When Indigenous peoples use the term nationhood, we aren't talking about nation states. We are talking about formations that respected and worked with different sovereignties over shared time and space. Giving up what you can so others might live. Again, this ethic of care.

It's the nation state as a delivery system for racial capitalism that's the problem. Racial capitalism requires borders and enclosures and violence. It requires heteropatriarchy and transphobia.

It is possible to make worlds that connect to other worlds, places where self-determination doesn't threaten the very viability of the planet where we can live and work together. It is possible to make Nishnaabeg places where we govern ourselves without the sort of borders. It is possible for living things to move and migrate without destroying Nishnaabeg homelands. There are lots of people from different moments and intellectual traditions dreaming and thinking about this. There are people in every part of the world coming together and building pieces of this with each other. Indigenous peoples on every content hold communal experiences and theory about how to live and live well without police, prisons and armies, in societies where violence is unthinkable, without enclosures.

10. This Time of Fires

We have been labouring to think what community, what being-together, looks and feels like, whether unfinished, attentive relationships conjure the conditions for political possibilities: where no one has to administer each other, where no one has to belong, where no one gets asked for their papers.

To be attentive to one another is to resist the work of the teleological, to be present and exposed in the everyday. That means being exposed to all of it, to all the unfamiliarities and incommensurableness and unfinishedness of being-together with people. And if we are working to extend friendship to the more-than-human, that means being exposed to all of it, to animals, insects, rivers, trees, fires and floods.

We are as fond of cute animal videos and spectacular sunsets as the next urbanite, but the more-than-human world is turbulent and unpredictable and very often violent and stomach-churning. It's comfortable enough to be exposed or attentive to an animal or mountain hike, but in search of a sensibility, a mode of friendship, we went in search of wildfires.

Fires are a regular feature of summers in the Pacific Northwest, but they have been accelerating in size and impact with global warming. We were curious about what being in close proximity to wildfires might do to our thinking, what it might disturb. We had written about fires in our previous book so we knew something of what we were heading for, but mostly went in blind this time, trying to learn how to be attentive.

We drove north from Vancouver (xʷməθkʷəyəm, səlilwəta and Skwxwú7mesh territories) up the Sea-to-Sky Highway, but as we drove, we were constantly reminded that we were passing through a wet, temperate rainforest. All of it, at least until St'at'imc territory, is saturated with water: pouring out of the skies through mist and fog, crashing down the steep slopes of the Coast Mountains through a dense forest of giant red cedars and Douglas firs dripping with mosses and ferns, cascading over, under and through the highway out into the Howe Sound fjord (Atl'ka7tsem).

Everything is wet out here: ocean on one side, rainforest on the other, and on most autumn days, rain pours out of the skies, streaming down through the mist and fog. On a typical British Columbia fall day your truck barrels from one pond-sized puddle after another, and with so much water on the left, the right and above, the main goal is usually to get inside and get dry. This wet corner of the Pacific Northwest coast feels like about the last place that's ever going to burn.

That warm November day though, the Sea-to-Sky Highway was sparkling in all its spectacular photographic-grade scenery. The sun was bouncing off the white-capped waves out in the Sound, the mountains were glowing with delicate frostings of snow and we were thinking about fire. It seemed impossible that this could burn, but all that summer, choked with smoke, trapped under a heat dome and crowded with pandemic paranoias, the threats of fire and heat never felt more real.

Up and down the west coast, from California to northern B.C., everything seemed to be burning that season. And it wasn't just here – unprecedented wildfires rampaged across Ontario and Siberia and Greece and Turkey and Brazil – flaming hellscapes searing images of climate catastrophes, creeping to the edges of major cities, often just barely or not-at-all controlled.

That heat-dome of 2021 sits in our memories like a smothering, sweaty fever-dream. We watched a homeless man literally fry an egg on a sidewalk. We repeatedly called 911, multiple times a day, for people felled by the heat, only to get put on hold. Emergency phone operators were overwhelmed – it often took 40 minutes just to get someone on the line, and then ambulances were triaging, telling people to do the best they could but 595 people in B.C. died directly from the heat. The streets were quiet, deserted of everyone who had anywhere cool to escape to. Even the birds were silent, all of us just trying to get through it.

Near the end of that hellish week, right in the maw of the heat, Lytton (Nlaka'pamux territory) found itself the object of international attention. A village of 250 or so people a few hours northeast of Vancouver, Lytton has always had hot summers, but trapped under the dome it was breaking historic marks. Global media breathlessly indexed its daily record-breaking: 115.9 degrees Fahrenheit on the 27th, 118.2 on the 28th, 121.3 on the 29th (that is 46.6, 47.9 and 49.6 degrees celsius). Three days in a row of the highest temperatures ever in Canada! Kind of unbelievably it got hotter here than it had *ever* been recorded in Las Vegas!

It was macabre, punishing entertainment: scorekeeping global heating in real-time. And then it went from gawking to horrified in a hot minute: a fire, sparked perhaps by a passing train, turbo-charged by the heat dome that had turned the entire town of Lytton to tinder. It started somewhere on the south end of town, and within 20 minutes flames had engulfed almost everything: homes, businesses, civic buildings. Everything was soon cinders. More than 1,000 people from the larger area had to flee with almost no notice. There was no evacuation, just a mad scramble to escape: north, south, east, anywhere to get out.

We had seen something like this before. In 2016 the two of us were writing a book about global warming and the tar sands of northern Alberta. We were in Ft. McMurray two months after the wildfires that caused 60,000 people to flee town. Without the wild heroism of firefighters and residents that whole city would have burned to the ground. Remarkably that town was substantively preserved, but witnessing the aftermath was still pretty startling.

We arrived in Ft. Mac a few weeks after the danger had passed and were shocked – not so much by the devastation, which we were mostly prepared for – but more by the asymmetries, the capriciousness, the speed, the bewildering patterns. We had kind of presumed that wildfires move like an ocean – a tide coming in steadily and then being beaten back – but it wasn't like that at all. Even after a ton of research and staring at maps with civic officials it was still confounding: the Ft. Mac fires were (at least to our eyes) so unpredictable – one house burned to bone-white remnants with the houses on either side untouched, one neighbourhood destroyed, the next one over entirely preserved: the fact that only two people died (while driving out) in those fires seems unimaginable, unduplicable.

The Lytton fire felt like the climate emergency finally landing in our own front yard, like waking to see nightmares come true: a world of heat and fires and accelerating losses, a slow-building anxiety attack now immediate and corporeal.

Most of us believe the decades-old science behind global warming to be true. Most of us understand and accept that anthropogenic climate change is a profound threat that must be met head-on and with urgency. But there is such a weird atemporality to global warming – demands to change right now for a world to come, a place and time far beyond our daily cadences, catastrophes possibly decades and continents away. What do numbers like 1.5 degrees or 425 ppm or 57 Gt/year mean when all you want to do is fly to some beach somewhere?

This damp place perched on the edge of the continent has always felt insulated from so much of the world: Far from major cities, British Columbia boasts a pleasantly moderate climate, robustly saturated with national delusions about Canadian virtues, ecological and otherwise. It has always felt like global warming was something that would hit somewhere else, somewhere far away, sometime after we're gone, something that doesn't involve us directly, yet.

Sometimes it feels like fundamental ecological transformation is within reach, other times it feels like we're stuck in a kind of frozen time where catastrophes are inevitable.

Some of us are doing vastly more than others to contribute to global warming. The colonial Canadian state remains aggressively wedded to oil-and-gas expansionism especially on Indigenous territories. Canadian Prime Minister Justin Trudeau has bailed out pipeline infrastructure and continues to claim that vast development of extractionism is the only route to a green future: "We must also continue to generate wealth from our abundant natural resources to fund this transition to a low-carbon economy."

This is precisely the contradiction so many of us find ourselves in. Grasping for a believably ecological future while hallucinating that we can get there with little pain. Does everything have to go up in flames first?

That's why we were headed for Lillooet (Tsilhqot'in, Statimc and Dënéndeh territories), Lytton (Nlaka'pamux territory), Merritt (Syilx and Nlaka'pamux territories), Penticton (Syilx territory) and some of the most fire-ravaged parts of the province. We were looking for something new, something to dislodge stuck notions, a future not on fire.

The journey from Vancouver to Lytton is spectacularly bifurcated. After the first couple hours of dense coastal rainforest, you get to Lil'Wat and turn onto the Duffey Lake Road, which heads straight up, switch-backing over and through the mountains and then boom! everything changes in an instant. You cross into an entirely different ecosystem. One minute you're on the cool, wet coast, the next you are in the hot, high, dry, semi-arid farm and ranch country of the B.C. interior.

We spent the night in Lillooet and then headed down to Lytton, about an hour southeast, the same place we had hiked with our beloved dog-friend. We were bracing ourselves, and it was exactly as we feared. The main strip of town is only about a half-mile long and remained open to traffic, but the road was straddled by high fencing blocking off all the side streets. Huge signs at each end of town implored you to keep your windows up due to the severe toxicity in the air, water and soil; stopping was prohibited. Security guards were posted at both ends of the strip to prevent gawking, so we had to make a half-dozen runs back and forth, crawling along and maybe occasionally getting out to look more closely and take photos. No one hassled us, but it did feel awkward and insensitive, staring at the remnants of a burned village.

One of our most glaring initial observations was that it was not a forest fire. It really just burned the town down. The fire razed the village in twenty minutes. But it did not jump the Thompson nor the Fraser River, which border the town to the west and north, and by the looks of it, the flames barely crossed the highway to the east. Residents blame the train. Lytton is a train town and the tracks run right through. A spark might have set the whole thing off. Videos posted on social media showed a train smoking as it went through Boston Bar, two hours south, that same day. The Transportation Safety Board conducted an investigation and then issued a statement assuring the public that it was not trains that sparked the fire.

Gordon Murray, a Lytton resident whose intense footage of the fire and his escape was splashed across international media, told us he could hear helicopters dropping water right in town. He said nearly half the residents didn't have insurance, himself included. He argued that if the town is to be rebuilt, it needs to have a different vision that brings together Indigenous and settler communities in a better way than existed before – one that, from a design and planning perspective, accounts for the reality of more climate-related disasters to come in the near future.

There is a bewildering array of competing interests at play even in a tiny village. Many folks wanted to move back in as quickly as possible – they were tired of shacking up in motels and spare rooms far from home, wondering who was going to pay for what. Some people were back rebuilding almost immediately, hoping that concrete houses will survive the next time around. The town council formally partnered with the Lytton First Nation to develop a fire-resistant recovery plan, but there are five Indigenous communities in the immediate area, many of whom propose alternative plans. Officials with the provincial preparedness program FireSmart urged patience and new "fire-ready" practices like "vegetation management," landscaping "only with fire-resistant species of trees, shrubs, plants and grasses," isolating firewood and propane far away from buildings, building comprehensive community evacuation plans and installing emergency speakers on trees and poles.

Surely residents should be at the heart of the decision-making; Lytton is a deeply meaningful place for so many people near and far. Maybe the fire is an opportunity to dramatically rethink the community. The town has been a colonial settlement since the 19th-century gold rush, built on traditional Indigenous territory. There are relationships between communities both human and other-than that could be explored in a meaningful way, to mend some of the wounds and missteps of the past and present, to prepare for a future very different from the way we live now. Does anyone think that heat dome was an anomaly that will never repeat itself?

We spoke to a number of senior firefighting professionals, and every one was open and frank about how dramatically the fires and floods continue to grow more destructive across B.C. New patterns of fire behavior throw into disarray all conventional response methods. Hotter, dryer summers scramble the ability to prepare. Fires that used to take three or four weeks to develop now explode suddenly and ferociously. It's obvious that where fire-fighting was once mostly a summer activity now has to be a year-round project.

There is a consensus emerging across North America among progressive fire officials, ecologists and conservation groups that a century of aggressive fire suppression has created a "fire paradox." As firefighting practices and resources grow in sophistication and effectiveness, the vast majority of fires are extinguished very quickly – but this leaves huge amounts of unburned land and flammable material left behind. This constantly accumulating stockpile presents a huge danger: When a fire does get out of control, it has vast amounts of organic material waiting, already primed and dried by the heat of global warming. This creates disastrous conditions for big fires to become catastrophic fires. The paradox is that there are now way too many fires and not nearly enough fires.

This is of course something that Indigenous people across the continent have been saying forever: that 'good fires' are incredibly important for ecological integrity and occasional burns are an essential part of the ecosystem. Forest fires burn clean and allow for regenerations. Indigenous nations all across British Columbia, all through the regions that have burned out of control in recent years, have always practised 'cultural burns' to protect their lands and communities.

We spent that night at our pals' Jeff and Sabine's cabin up the Nahatlatch River, arguing late about whether humans can be friends with animals, or a tree, or the river: "If friends are supposed to be always there for you, I feel like that tree has been here for me, shading this cabin, for more than forty years now. It feels like a friend" Jeff said that night. We wondered if the tree could or would possibly reciprocate.

The next day we drove over to Penticton (Syilx/Okanagan Nation Alliance Territory including the Sn/Pink/tn), four and a half hours east. That day and the next we criss-crossed through the South Okanagan region, past wildfires that were still burning, had recently been extinguished or had caused major disruptions and evacuations through the summer. The Okanagan is the hot, dry south-central area of British Columbia, famed for lakefront hoatels, fruit-growing, pocket deserts, often-punishing heat and, in recent years, relentless wildfires.

As we drove over and through the Okanagan past many major fire sites, it all still felt wildly flammable, even deep into autumn. Essentially all the major fires were extinguished or under control, but it was still so parched. It is a profoundly different ecosystem from the coast, all tumbleweeds and gnarled ponderosa pines, now riddled with orchards and wineries and garish gated retirement developments. It reminds many people of the Mediterranean – Lebanese, Turks, southern Italians and Croatians often say it feels like home. We drove up to the site of the most damaging wildfire in B.C. history – the 2003 Okanagan Mountain Park Fire, which forced out 33,000 residents – and wondered how the hell another fire up here could ever be controlled.

It is now orthodox analysis that the whole South Okanagan is threatened by fire year after year due to unecological forest practices and fire management.

Prominent Indigenous voices here have long clamored that if the province had listened to them – had adopted, understood or even recognized long-standing Indigenous fire prevention strategies – these wildfires would be manageable and far less fearsome. "Forests have been mismanaged for over 100 years," elected Member of the Legislative Assembly of BC Joan Phillip, told us. "Cultural fires need to be part of the solution."

That summer underlined just how intensely the domination of humans and the domination of the other-than-human world are entwined. Coloniality violently suppresses not just human bodies and subjectivities, but knowledges, ways of being. In the same breath, it both builds ferocious dysfunctions and forecloses possible routes out.

Does friendship offer any break in these clouds, is it a disposition that can surpass domination, gesture at another anti-colonial way of being in the world? We have been labouring hard to think past borders, but also to let our thinking remain unfinished, incomplete. A cultural burn might not feel all that friendly to a tree, but it might well to the forest as a whole. Could we ever be friends with the more-than-human world?

11. The Capture of Time

We returned home after that week of fire-chasing still unsure of ourselves. It was perfect weather for writing: cool and rainy, ideal for staying inside, sitting by the fire. And then it just didn't stop raining. This is standard-grade coastal British Columbia fall weather – the rain locks in relentlessly for weeks at a time – but this was something different. The rain was heavy, and then got heavier, and then it got ugly.

Turns out we were in the middle of an 'atmospheric river' – a designation very few of us had ever heard of before – but was eerily descriptive. That's exactly what it felt like – the rain wasn't just coming down, it was all around, dumping a month's worth of rain in just two days. And then things got worse: the river-in-the-sky triggered landslides, vast flooding, dykes overflowing and mass evacuations all across the southwest of B.C.

Soon after we returned, the province declared yet another state of emergency, including travel restrictions and fuel rationing as supply lines were broken, all major highways and rail lines heading east were severed, and Vancouver was cut off from the rest of Canada.

The main devastation traced the exact route we traveled the week previous. Five people were killed on the Duffey Road by mudslides. Lillooet was swamped and people were still missing. All 7100 residents of Merritt were evacuated on short notice. The wastewater system was overwhelmed, and raw sewage flooded the waters as the main bridges out of town failed. People were told to go to Kamloops if their home address was odd-numbered and Kelowna if their address was even-numbered. Those places are between an hour and two hours away if the roads are clear. The roads were not clear. Agricultural communities all through the Fraser Valley saw hundreds of thousands of farm animals drowned.

All of a sudden, our bland little corner of the world, where most people presume almost nothing ever happens, was making global headlines yet again. Friends were calling from all over wondering if we were ok and what the hell was going on. Those few months felt biblical, end-of-times: back-to-back-to-back states of emergency, one catastrophe after another, each exacerbating the previous one.

The floods of course were intimately connected to the fires. Mismanaged forests burn hotter and wilder than ever before, stripping the forest floor of the vegetation that soaks up water. These super-hot fires create hydrophobic (water-repellent) crusts on the soil, so that water cannot be absorbed and runs freely on the surface. Then waters rushing downhill add excess sediment and debris to rivers, reducing room for water, accelerating overflows, eroding banks and adding to property damage as rushing water bounces detritus off anything in its path. It feels like we have entered an ecological spiral, with one calamity triggering the next. The fantasy of borders, of imagining that somehow the performative enforcement of state territory is a realistic form for being together, for living through ecological crises, has never been more absurd.

Ursula K. Le Guin called freedom "that recognition of each person's solitude which alone transcends it"[1] and if nothing else, the pandemic taught us that none of us are alone, none of our bodies are exclusively ours. Our breath is your breath, we share viruses and water and air and land, humans and more-than-humans alike. We suffer alone, but that suffering, that exposure to grief, is maybe the only way we might be together.

All through that winter the water kept coming. More episodic floods rose and fell across British Columbia and of course, the water cared little for the border. In Washington State, record-breaking levels of rain and snow closed major highways, residents of several towns north of Seattle were forced to flee severe flooding and Governor Jay Inslee issued an emergency proclamation due to winter storms. And still the

---

1   Ursula K. Le Guin, The Dispossessed, New York: Harper and Row, 1974. 300.

atmospheric rivers flowed, arriving one after the other, exacerbated by startling high tides. In Seattle more than one early January tide was two feet higher than forecast: the highest ever documented in Puget Sound through more than a century of record-keeping.

The inundation was hardly unique to the Pacific Northwest, nor to that winter. Flooding and sea-level rise is one of the central features of climate change, and places across the globe are experiencing regular and unprecedented flood-events, from above and below. From Katrina to New York subways to the walls of water crashing into Zhengzhou to Pakistan to Burkina Faso, it's hard to find anywhere that hasn't been struggling though the 21st Century, swimming against the tides of flooding and historic levels of precipitation.

Global warming is obviously a prime culprit here: melting glaciers, wild rainstorms, newly unpredictable tides, destabilized weather are all part of a planet off-kilter. But disastrous flooding has always haunted humans. Everywhere, and all through history, there are horrific stories of rivers overflowing their banks, rushing through cities, drowning fields, bringing disease and famine. Some of these disasters are almost unimaginable in scale, causing millions of deaths and reshaping whole topographies.

But floods are also considered a regular blessing in many places. The flooding of the Nile is worthy of annual celebration – *Wafaa El-Nil* – the overflowing of its banks has been central to agricultural fertility for millennia. The Fertile Crescent was created by the Tigris and Euphrates, nutrient-rich American floodplains by the Mississippi spilling silt onto fields. Every river has adjacent ecological zones that are predicated on regular flooding, and people have always had to be attentive not just to the dangers but the blessings of floods, shaping and managing flows in something akin to relationships with 'good fires'.

Floods are of course also closely bound to metaphorical and spiritual narratives of end-times, of the washing away of enmities, of godly retributions and of rebirth. Stories of pissed-off deities punishing sinful people with floods are startlingly common. From Masai to Sumerian to Roman to Zhuang to Batak, essentially every culture – Indigenous and non – has deeply-embedded stories of the earth being cleansed by water. These stories frequently feature a wooden boat or island filled with survivors to repopulate the land. Alternatively, or in combination, flood stories are often those of one brave person – a child or animal – desperately trying to warn people to flee the coming waters, only to be ignored.

These are not only old stories. This general sweep is eerily redolent of many renditions of global warming, with human sin being washed away by a Gaianistic deity finally irritated beyond all patience, and a few brave souls helplessly trying to alert us to the danger.

End-times stimulate rhetorical flourishes, and it's no wonder that water remains maybe the most heavily drawn upon well of cliches. Whether it's Bruce Lee demanding we 'be like water' or some right-wing hack brandishing images of their precious nation being swamped by 'floods of immigrants' instigating 'waves of crime', water is equated with fluidity, passing, travel, and rebirth.

If Hannah Arendt said that all politics rest on movement, maybe we can renovate her claim to suggest that it is *water* that is "the substance and meaning of all things political." If water is closely tied to notions of freedom and release – from dreamy, time-free vacations by the ocean to flowing away on a boat – water is equally used as a border guard. Whether it is Mexicans wading the Rio Grande, Africans in rafts trying to get across the Mediterranean, Rohingyas swimming the Naf River trying to get into Bangladesh, or the bodies of Syrian children washing up in the waves on Greek islands, water is deployed as an instrument of violence and containment.

The idea that anything is fixed in place – spatially or temporally – is a particularly colonial pathology. Water defies all fixities in its very composition – it really is literally true that you can never step in the same river twice – and the command and control of water is always an extension of colonial spatial fantasy. If capitalism fetishizes the capture of time – what is a boss or a wage other than the command of time? – then the experience of water is precisely the fluid antagonist of capture.

The thrust of Bergsonian duration calls on imagination to grasp the unspooling of time that defies causal determinisms. Time flows river-like, enduring attempts to arrest and document it at specific junctures, and defying mechanistic interventions. Bergson's duree is precisely the notion that freedom and mobility are temporal as much spatial.

The spread of empire is not just the capture of space and territory, but the keeping of time, constrained within matrices of minutes, hours and weeks that can mark the march of productive progress. The production of coordinated GMT time produces specifically indexed ways of being in the world, suspending subjectivities into grids and google-calendars and synchronized schedules, but also pious demands for 'slowing down' or 'life-work balance' in this 'fast-moving' world, as if there was a single people-moving conveyor belt for which we just need to find the right modulation.

Conservation and conservatism speak to the same desires: to return the world to how it once was, to the 'good-old days' when everything and everyone was in its right place, to a timelessness that resisted movement. These warm evocations are the lingua franca of ethno-nationalists and racist environmentalists alike, preserving time and place in cocoons of surety. This same language permeates discourses of global warming with escalatingly shrill claims that 'time is running out', there are *these* thresholds and *that* timeline and *this* tipping point, with the only antidotes being new schedules and different timelines for 'sustainable' development.

But for *whom* and *what* is time 'running out'? The claims to 'emergency' after four-hundred years of genocide and empire and pillage and species collapse and ecological catastrophe often ring hollow. And what precisely is the world 'we' all have to scramble to save: current configurations of capital, debt, surplus labour value-extraction, patriarchy, etc.? Is the argument that if we can all mobilize to solve global warming, then we can sort the rest of all that out at some later date? As Claire Colebrook writes:

> Rather than follow Martin Heidegger who argues that an animal is "poor in world" – because its range of decision and potentiality does not harbor the sense of possibility of a radically free existence – it would be better to think of "world" as the horizon of what matters, with *some* versions of world producing the neoliberal values of privacy, autonomy, and individualism. "End of world" culture – from post-

apocalyptic cinema to daily press releases warning of *future* resource depletion and scarcity – presupposes the world of hyper-consumption in which each person is composed from a series of individual choices [...] Faced with the end of "the world" where all that matters appears to be this horizon of distinct life choices and in a milieu of privacy and personal decision, it is time to ask about what other worlds might be possible.[2]

Speculative futures are hardly the exclusive province of science fiction and critical theory. In December 2020 water futures were, for the first time, made available for trading. Launched by the Chicago Mercantile Exchange (CME), the first tranche of these commodified water contracts was limited to five districts in California but are surely the thin edge of the wedge. With this new market, traders can take a stake in the future value of water, and CME Group executive Tim McCourt speculates that pricing water risk will be a business that expands well beyond California. McCourt called the market "liquid and transparent" and noted that,"With nearly two-thirds of the world's population expected to face water shortages by 2025, water scarcity presents a growing risk for businesses and communities around the world."[3]

Seneca, quoting Epicurus, once said that "The fool, with all his other faults, has this also, he is always getting ready to live".[4] But there's just too much money lying around out there not to be looking just a little into the future, getting ready to profit on future disasters, water-saturated and otherwise. Speculation captures the future as powerfully as debt, and markets are very actively shaping and reshaping what other worlds might be possible.

If floods – like fires – are a constantly active agent remaking our worlds, predictably unpredictable, undercutting systemicities and ruining landscapes, is there an imagination that does not hate floods,

2   Claire Colebrook, The Personal and the Political, Women's Studies, 50:8, 805–811, 2021.

3   Don Pitts,' Can Wall Street help us find the true price of water?' CBC News, January 11th, 2021.

4   Maria Popova, 'A Stoic's Key to Peace of Mind', The Marginalian, August, 2017.

that does not spend every last possible resource trying to contain and suppress them? The question of how to be-together cannot restrict itself to just being with other humans, or even animals, plants, or what we imagine to be alive. Floods and fires are not our kin.

Nation, state, belonging and kinship have proven themselves wildly inadequate to the task of being-together, reconstituting the same idealized renditions of fixed identity in new guises, but there have to be possible worlds where floods and fires and all the rest of the more-than-human world are our friends.

12. A Borderless World

This book has been animated by a desire to imagine a borderless world where humans and the more-than-human can move freely, think and be together. A time when no one is pushed back into the sea. The current political moment clearly demarcates a planetary-scale intensification, a hardening of movement and a thickly-bordered political imaginary. Psycho-spatial politics, assemblages of infrastructure, myriad surveillance technologies and the production of ordering regimes of fear create zones of permanent administration from which none of us are exempt.

As Hagar Kotef notes in her book *The Colonizing Self,* Arendt saw placelessness as a crisis. Refugees lost "the right to stay, to take place, to reside and with it the ability to form community[...]"[1] The right to have rights is conditioned on the right to be placed with others in proximity. Without the wall of the polis or the boundaries to convey who has rights within a political community, the very formation of the political community is at risk. So, in the present time, the delineation of boundaries, fences, enclosures is touted as part of the 'stability' required for a precondition of politics. But the originary violence of the spatial demarcation of territory is never fully sublimated. The political tension reappears again and again as the formation of community remains irresolvable and irresolute.

If we are to adequately think past the colonial fixities of nationalist thinking, between the preservation and thriving of life and the earth in a planetary sense, we offer that friendship allows a possible route out from

---

1   Hagar Kotef, The Colonizing Self: Or, Home and Homelessness in Israel/ Palestine. Durham: Duke University Press, 2020, 58.

this closure. A borderless world is possible where a revolutionary politics runs through constantly unfinished exposure: a vitalist politics that speaks to solidarities with the more-than-human. The adjudication of ecological crises is currently contained primarily inside the human: if we can acknowledge the creativity and subjectivities of the more-than-human world, a new possibility of the political emerges. As Mbembe writes:

> The Earth's specificity lies in that it makes room for all its inhabitants, with no distinction of race or species. It mocks both the blind particular and the bare singularity. It reminds us of how each body, human or otherwise, however singular, bears on it and within it, in its essential porosity, not the marks of the universal, but traces of the in-common. As a result, every politics of the living rests, by definition, on the idea that the living is that which is priceless. And because it is priceless, it is fundamentally beyond measure. As such, it can neither be counted nor weighed. It belongs simply, to the incalculable.[2]

The idea that without strong borders you cannot have a strong nation is precisely the closure that has to be challenged in order to consider a new way of being in the world. Through this porosity, we rediscover the essence of politics and its reinvigoration.

The permanent administration and intricacies of human and more-than-human mobility characterizes our global present. This is a time of accelerating planetary entanglement for structural reasons: a combination of late-capitalism, hyper-technological forms of warfare, digital surveillance, planetary-scale computation and acceleration of speed. These phenomena produce new forms and possibilities of exposure and tension points of border zones. To be inextricably bound with the other is a technical and pragmatic reality, and one we are forced to critically grapple with. The price of abandoning those who are relegated to surplus life is to banish them to the carceral space of colonial boundaries and border controls.

---

2   Achille Mbembe, The Earthly Community: Reflection on the Last Utopia. V2 Publishing, 2022, 34.

It is in the possibility of sharing our fate with others, by opening our borders to fight for a world in common, that politics can take its proper form. There is a moral and ecological imperative to rethink democracy beyond the human, to do away with the absurdity of the state being the guarantor and protector of community. A borderless world presupposes a shared fate as a precondition for its durability and existential viability. A death in the Mediterranean, a migrant crossing the Texas border, an Afghani without status, or a Uygur in China, are bound together as much as floods and fires bind us to one another. Brute conditions unravel into a world degenerating upon itself in elemental indifferences.

The various forms of extractivist capitalism and its ordering mechanisms turbo-boosted by state policy capture are the perfect dead-end vicious circle that we find ourselves in. When the future is mortgaged to a trajectory of planetary collapse and perishability, time stands still waiting for economic and civilizational disorder. It can produce either a nihilism or accelerationist orientation that undermines political agency in the present. It models a futurity that asks nothing of people but to wait quietly in the corner for the catastrophe-to-come.

How can sociality be borderless and private property abandoned? How can we move from the insularity of a given community to an assemblage of a becoming public? In this time of planetary nihilism and the foreclosure of being that it intimates and gestures toward, can a sweetness of living open up a horizon beyond the exhaustions of present-day politics? How can a relationship between inoperativity and destituent potential be forged? What are the modes of intervention to overcome the civil war between human and animal, beast and sovereign, that exists inside every being? Within the localization of the disaster, violence destroys language and transforms conditions of the possible into an unspeakable community.[3]

We submit that through friendship, it is possible to apprehend a world where trees can speak, a rock can dance, a starling can turn with the flock, a fish can pivot with a school and a dog can cut an umbilical

---

3   See artist Grace Euna Kim's 'Unspeakable Community' project.

cord after giving birth. Our current crises can never be solved by borders – they can only consolidate, and exacerbate dead-end orientations and structured forms of domination. Establishing a durability for our collective planetary existence is to abandon some parts of ourselves, to share the impossibility and absurdity of existing in a self that is bound to the existence of another, an openness that remains open, always unfinished.

To be *with* is to be inside of a world that belongs in the space of proximity and porosity, both mysterious and intimate. That capacity to touch, to make and remake the world with humans, trees, rocks and animals, is the place where friendship forms the basis of politics.

Even if the barriers, barricades and borders remain, we must think over, through and around them to the site of a new possibility. In this political moment, where the closures and exhaustions of thought are all around us, the refusal to be enemies, to imagine a borderless world where the human and more-than human can correspond, touch, feel, think, love and congregate is precisely to open up a political space of friendship where it is possible to think of a proper freedom for all and imagine together the preservation of collective life in an interstitial zone of irresponsibility. When the nature of time takes on new meanings, when the immanence of truths is a work never completed but always open and moving, a borderless world beyond language and dreams is possible.

Love and friendship are bound up with precarious vulnerability. The potent durability of a contingent 'we' is based around the premise that a community may no longer exist in time. The binding relation is not a legal commitment but the mutual creation of a solidarity beyond the law – moving from *being-with* to *being-for*.

All living things, human and more-than-human, conceive and conspire towards an existence beyond recognition that collectively is a story of the living. Plants, bacteria, skies, clouds, lakes, flora, fauna, rocks, mountains, cheetahs and reptiles. Conceiving of a future that includes all is an opening to imagine friendship and community beyond the limits of the human and the planetary technological frame. To render possible a shared dignity is to separate ourselves from the inheritances of human-centred lines of thought and embrace the multitude of possible futures. The mutations of subjectivity, and possibilities of dissolution, that come to the surface when the perishability of the earth and its life forms is made visible, ask for new doors and thresholds at the closures of the emerging frontlines where community is made durable through constant exposure.

There is an unaccountability of accelerated time that closes in on itself through the proliferation of fires, floods, displacements and artificial intelligence careening beyond human or technological control. The right to move becomes non-negotiable as a site of existential preservation. To imagine a world beyond borders and the extension of a carceral landscape is to be inside the reflexive plasticity of dwelling on the earth. As Mbembe argues, to overcome the architecture of violence that functions at a planetary scale, there is a call to be attuned to the constitutive fragility of the critical zones of life and their places of encounter and entanglement that form the basis of a possible resistance amongst different forms-of-life.[4]

It is through the assembling of practices by which living beings and the more-than-human cohabitate with friendship and hazard the tenuous formation of communities. The return to mutuality, transformative solidarity, the recognition of our planetary vulnerability beyond the limits of reactionary human identities is a call to collectively reinvigorate our existence in the time that remains, to build proximity to a seemingly impossible justice. The organizing of a series of ruptures towards a new life is to think around the inherited order and open the door to the potency and poetry of new thresholds, through visible and invisible solidarities, where the creative mutations of politics can form promiscuous alliances that surpass contemporary thresholds and modes of the possible.

---

4   Notes adapted from Achille Mbembe's seminar on 'The Last Utopia' in Saas Fee at the European Graduate School in July 2023.

Bibliography

Agamben, Giorgio (2009): 'The Friend', in What is an Apparatus?, Stanford University Press.

Agamben, Giorgio (1993): The Coming Community, University of Minnesota Press.

Ahmed, Sarah, (2013): Feminist Killjoys: Making Feminist Points: https://feministkilljoys.com/2013/09/11/making-feminist-points/.

An Open Letter to Elizabeth Warren' (2020): https://medium.com/@ewarrenisnotcherokee/open-letter-to-elizabeth-warren-from-cherokee-citizens-ab053578bd95.

Anderson, Benedict (1983): Imagined Communities: Reflections on the Origin and Spread of Nationalism, Verso.

Blanchot, Maurice (2006): The Unavowable Community, Station Hill Press.

Boyden, Joseph (2017): 'My name is Joseph Boyden', in Macleans Magazine, macleans.ca/news/canada/my-name-is-joseph-boyden/

Buna, M. (2018): 'Why Still Look at Animals: A Conversation with OxanaTimofeeva', in LA Review of Books, https://lareviewofbooks.org/article/why-still-look-at-animals-a-conversation-with-oxana-timofeeva/.

Butler, Judith (2002): Is Kinship Always Already Heterosexual?, in A Journal of Feminist Cultural Studies, 13.1.

Butler, Judith (2021): The Force of Non-Violence, Verso.

Colebrook, Claire (2021): The Personal and the Political, in Women's Studies, 50:8, 805–811.

Dean, Jodi (2019): Comrade: An Essay on Politcal Belonging, Verso.

Deleuze, Gilles/Guattari, Felix (1987): A Thousand Plateaus: Capitalism and Schizophrenia, University of Minnesota Press.

Derrida, Jacques (1997): The Politics of Friendship, Verso.

Gandhi, Leela (2006): Affective Communities, Duke University Press.

Gandhi, Leela (2014): The Common Cause, University of Chicago Press.

Geddes, Linda (2014): 'There is no DNA test to prove you're Native American' in NewScientist. https://www.newscientist.com/article/mg221 29554-400-there-is-no-dna-test-to-prove-youre-native-american/.

Govindrajan, Radhika (2018): Animal Intimacies, University of Chicago Press.

Haraway, Donna (2016): Staying With the Trouble, Duke University Press.

Haraway, Donna (2007): When Species Meet, University of Minnesota Press.

Haider, Asad (2022): Mistaken Identity, Verso.

Kotef, Hagar (2020): The Colonizing Self, Duke University Press.

Kotef, Hagar (2015): Movement and the Ordering of Freedom, Duke University Press.

Le Guin, Ursula K. (1974): The Dispossessed, Harper and Row.

Manning, Dolleen Tisawii'ashii, (2017): "The Murmuration of Birds: An Anishinaabe Ontology of Mnidoo-Worlding." in Feminist Phenomenology Futures, Eds. Helen Fielding and Dorothea Olkowski. Bloomington In: Indiana University Press.

Massumi, Brian (2014): What Animals Teach Us About Politics, Duke University Press.

Mbembe, Achille (2019): Necropolitics, Duke University Press.

Mbembe, Achille (2022): The Earthly Community, V2 Publishing.

Mbembe, Achille (2023): seminar on 'The Last Utopia' in Saas Fee at the European Graduate School.

McMaster, Geoff (2018): 'Indigenous DNA no proof of Indigenous identity, says Native studies scholar', University of Alberta, Folio. https://www.ualberta.ca/folio/2018/11/indigenous-dna-no-proo f-of-indigenous-identity-says-native-studies-scholar.html.

Milman, Oliver (2021): 'Right-Wing Climate Denial Is Being Replaced – by Nativism', in Mother Jones. https://www.motherjones.com/polit

ics/2021/11/right-wing-climate-denial-anti-immigrant-nativism-m igration/.

Morgan, Ryan (2019): 'Trump at UN: 'The future does not belong to globalists. The future belongs to patriots.' American Military News. https://americanmilitarynews.com/2019/09/trump-at-un-the-futu re-does-not-belong-to-globalists-the-future-belongs-to-patriots/.

Nagle, Rebecca (2019): 'Elizabeth Warren Has Spent Her Adult Life Repeating a Lie. I Want Her to Tell The Truth.' In HuffPost. https:// www.huffpost.com/entry/elizabeth-warren-cherokee-apology_n_5 d5ed7e6e4b0dfcbd48a1b01.

Nancy, Jean-Luc (1991): The Inoperative Community. University of Minnesota Press.

Nancy, Jean-Luc (2016): The Disavowed Community, Fordham University Press.

Nussbaum, Martha (2023): Justice for Animals, New York: Simon and Schuster.

Paulson, Steve (2019) 'Making Kin: An Interview with Donna Haraway, in LA Review of Books.'

Pitts, Don (2021): 'Can Wall Street help us find the true price of water?' in CBC News. https://www.cbc.ca/news/business/water-futures-pr ice-1.5866538.

Popova, Maria (2017): 'A Stoic's Key to Peace of Mind'. https://www.them arginalian.org/2017/08/27/seneca-anxiety/.

Sharpe, Christina (2016): 'Lose Your Kin', in The New Inquiry. https://the newinquiry.com/lose-your-kin/.

Sherwood, Harriet (2022): 'Choosing pets over babies is 'selfish and diminishes us', says Pope', in The Guardian. https://www.theguardi an.com/world/2022/jan/05/pope-couples-choose-pets-children-sel fish.

Simpson, Audra (2014): Mohawk Interruptus: Political Life Across the Borders of Settler States, Duke University Press.

Simpson, Leanne (2013): Islands of Decolonial Love, Arbeiter Ring.

Simpson, Leanne (2017): This Accident of Being Lost: Astoria.

Simpson, Leanne (2020): As We Have Always Done, University of Minnesota Press.

Torpey, John (2018): The Invention of the Passport, Cambridge University Press.

Verkerk, Willow (2019): Nietzsche and Friendship, Bloomsbury.

Walia, Harsha (2013): Undoing Border Imperialism, AK Press.

[transcript]

PUBLISHING. KNOWLEDGE. TOGETHER.

transcript publishing stands for a multilingual transdisciplinary pro-gramme in the social sciences and humanities. Showcasing the latest academic research in various fields and providing cutting-edge diagno-ses on current affairs and future perspectives, we pride ourselves in the promotion of modern educational media beyond traditional print and e-publishing. We facilitate digital and open publication formats that can be tailored to the specific needs of our publication partners.

OUR SERVICES INCLUDE

- partnership-based publishing models
- Open Access publishing
- innovative digital formats: HTML, Living Handbooks, and more
- sustainable digital publishing with XML
- digital educational media
- diverse social media linking of all our publications

Visit us online: www.transcript-publishing.com

Find our latest catalogue at www.transcript-publishing.com/newbookspdf

GPSR Authorized Representative: Easy Access System Europe, Mustamäe tee
50, 10621 Tallinn, Estonia, gpsr.requests@easproject.com

* 9 7 8 3 8 3 7 6 7 0 2 6 4 *